Olson's Penny Arcade

OLSON'S PENNY ARCADE

Poems by Elder Olson

University of Chicago Press

Chicago and London

For permission to reprint poems which first appeared in their pages, the author wishes to thank the editors of *The Chicago Review, First Stage, The New Yorker,* and *The Virginia Quarterly Review.*

The University of Chicago Press, Chicago 60637
The University of Chicago Press, Ltd., London
© *1963, 1975 by Elder Olson*
All rights reserved. Published 1975
Printed in the United States of America
79 78 77 76 75   987654321

Library of Congress Cataloging in Publication Data

Olson, Elder, 1909–
    Olson's penny arcade.
    I. Title. II. Title: Penny arcade.
PS3529.L66P4   1975   811'.5'2   75–5080
ISBN 0–226–62893–0

In memory of my beloved friends
Ann, William, and Bernard Weinberg

The star is dead
Its light lives on

Contents

Prefatory Note

With one exception, the poems in this book are a selection from pieces composed after the publication of my *Collected Poems*. The exception is the Munich piece, written in the year designated in its title and inspired—if that is the right word—by the events of that year.

If these poems range from jocosity to fury and near-suicidal despair, that is because they reflect the kind of person I happen to be and the world we happen to live in. The poet who finds it necessary to explain his work tacitly admits that he has failed in some way; I am willing to make no such admission, but perhaps a note or two will be useful to you. The first of the "Four Immensely Moral Tales" is drawn from *The Panchatantra*; I have, however, made some changes, and I find a quite different moral implied in it. The third is based upon a poem I read nearly fifty years ago in a magazine called, I believe, *Deutscher Welt-Humor*. In the German poem the elephant did not believe in violets. I cannot recall the author's name, but I still remember certain lines: "Es war einmal ein Elefant / Der wollte nicht an Veilchen glauben"; confronted with the evidence, the elephant disposed of it in the manner of my beast, remarking, "Veilchen gibt es nicht." If my hero in his mode of disputation reminds you of Dr. Samuel Johnson, who derided James Bruce's accurate accounts of Africa and who dealt with Berkeley's philosophy by stamping his foot and saying, "I refute it thus!"—so be it; that is Johnson's fault, not mine. The other two moral tales are of my own invention.

The title poem is a single work, although it appears to be a mere sequence. The technique used is similar to the Connect-A-Dot games that amuse children; the individual poems are the dots, and if you trouble to connect them, they construct a picture of a man worrying about the chief things that worry all of us. The epigraph comes from an anecdote of Danny Kaye's, in which men of various nationalities state what they conceive happiness to be; the Russian tells them that happiness consists in discovering that the secret police have not come for him but for Ivan who lives on the next floor. Number XVII, called "Olson's Theory of Relativity," is simply my version of an old Arab proverb.

Many of the images in the poem on Tomlinson's *The Sea and the Jungle* are taken from that book. Originally I set them in quotation marks, then in italics, but found such devices cumbersome and distracting. If, in order to determine the precise degree of my indebtedness, you are induced to read that enchanting book, so much the better for you.

ONE

The Daguerreotype of Chopin

Et mon art, où a-t-il passé? Et mon coeur, où l'ai-je galvaudé?
. . . Le monde s'évanouit autour de moi de manière tout à fait étrange
—je me perds—je n'ai plus aucune force.
Je me sens seul, seul, seul . . .

Huddled in a heavy coat, as if shivering
Even indoors in the Parisian spring,
Haggard, faintly frowning,

Incuriously you peer—not the Chopin
Of caricature or portrait, but the living, dying man:
Blanched collar, dark cravat,

Long locks, the strange hair of the sick,
The arched nose shadowing hollow cheek
And feebly parted lips,

The frail strong famous hands
Chalk-white, crossed as if to hint
At the not remote event,

All still, until a little patience should
Make momentary stillness absolute.
Then, too, despair itself has its own quietude.

On the draped taboret at which you do not look
Lies an unsuspected
Omen: a closed book.

You sit indifferent, haughty, neat;
On your flesh all but drained of blood,
Almost visibly, vampires feed.

Son of your century, you
Were haunted like Baudelaire, like Poe:
What summoned you to go

Down midnight galleries
Eavesdropping on cries
And clangors from the Abyss?

Was it wise,
Trespassing on Paradise?
Could this world not suffice?

The blood fretted in your veins
Till you turned all senses into one,
Enchanting into tone

Feel
Of velvet, steel,
Sun's warmth, moon's chill,

Smart of poisons, fever of wines,
Rose-color, -form, -fragrance,
Sound even of silence,

And all the Romantic's images:
Mist-bound fragile palaces,
Ships in curled fantastic seas,

Trophies of ancient loves and wars,
And of course
The fashionable objects of crypt and charnel house.

What empery, sorcerer,
Was yours, upon what terms,
Over the wild worlds of air!

—When Poland fell, you made
Out of your sacked and burning heart
The Poland no enemy could invade.

Here the priceless gift at last
Reveals its terrifying cost,
Body and soul laid waste.

Would all that melody in its delicate ornament
Have gone unheard unless a man were warped and bent
Like the viol's wood, to be its instrument?

4

And is such suffering, such blight
Needful to such beauty, then
As to the nightingale the night?

—Then what powers, demonic or divine,
Curse, bless in one touch, wreck the mortal man
To build the immortal from his ruin?

Or are god and demon one?

Souvenir of the Play

Unrehearsed, our pretty play
Began on the bare wintry stage;
All the loves of all the ages
Told us what to do and say.
We spoke, and the first syllable
Was the kiss that woke the spring,
Enchanted sleeper, from her spell;
The next, the pilgrim's miracle
Of dead branches blossoming.
We asked what season could destroy
This, that turned winter into spring:
How should this end except in joy,
This, all happy tales made one,
With no more ending than a tale
Ending to be told again?

In autumn's ruined theater
We kept forgetting toward the end.
We heard the promptings of the wind
But these were from a different play.
The crumbling and discolored scene
Fell rag by rag and blew away;
White as plaster the grotesque
Moon hung like a tragic mask.
We stopped and listened to the wind,
We stared and had no more to say.

Munich: New Year's Eve, 1936

Winter trims gable, hutch, and stair,
Railing and sill in its cheap fur.
Westward, gloom extinguishes
The last spire in its tinsel snow.
The lamps wear saffron haloes now

—False-looking-Christmas-card-like scene
All spangled fluff and glitter-dust—
But the vague figures moving here
Through clouds of snow and fogs of dusk
Look and act like living men

And so indeed I thought them once.
I had friends here, as I believed.
I comprehend Hoffmann's disgust
Finding Olympia, whom he loved,
Only an automaton.

Once the will is given away
The soul itself will never stay,
A form remains, and that is all.
These are not humankind, with souls,
But merely clockwork-driven dolls

(A simple mechanism, too:
Mainspring of greed, checktooth of fear)
Like the mannikins in their clock-tower
Who strut forth at each striking hour
Till Death comes round to end the show.

Their honor lies in rubbish-bins,
Their future may lie there as well
For—quaint as such clockwork may appear—
There have been greater marvels still:
It is not many decades since

Their emperor owned a comfit-box
Whereon, with the small lid for stage,
Horse, soldiery, rabble, tiny king
Enacted a town's furious siege
—Rubbish, when someone broke the spring.

I tell them this before I go
—Doubtless the last truth they will hear:
A darker season still draws near
And more will finish than a year
And in the fall of more than snow.

Nightfall

The mist-foot man who forms within my cellars,
Steals fog-like from my drains, to stalk my slums,
Unguessed by those who stroll my boulevards;

The midnight man who rises at my nightfalls,
Walks in my sleep, takes substance from my shadows,
To stand beyond my street-lamps, dressed in dark,

Stirs again, creeps up his secret stair.

Is he my shadow, or am I his mask?
Which of us is the real? In dread to know

I drive him to his dungeon-pits, where I
Myself fall prisoner, while he keeps the key.

I cannot rise till he ascends his towers,
I move in darkness till he finds his light.

The Mad Priest of the Mountain

"The farmer nailed the shot hawk, not quite dead,
To the barn-door; it hangs here, wings outspread.
Keep your carved Christs on crossed sticks;
I take this for my crucifix,"
The mad priest of the mountain said.

"Christ's fault was to fall foul of the wrong lot;
The hawk's, to venture within rifle-shot.
Puzzle till you burst your brain;
What pain means is pain, pain;
We give it meanings it has not."

Directions for Building a House of Cards

This is a house of cards. To build this house
You must have patience, and a steady hand.
That is the difficulty. You must have a steady hand
No matter what has happened, and unless something has
   happened
You will not care to build this house of cards.

And you must have cards, enough to tell your fortune
Or make your fortune, but to build this house
You must see all fortunes merely as so many cards,
Differing, no doubt, but not for you.
You must know this, and still keep a steady hand.

And you must have patience, and nothing better to do
Than to make this toy because it was your way
To make a toy of fortune, which was not your toy,
Until at last you have nothing better to do
Than to build this final thing with nothing inside,

Fool's work, a monument to folly, but built with difficulty
Because everything is difficult once you understand
That after what has been, nothing can be
But things like this, with nothing inside, like you.
You must see this, and somehow keep a steady hand.

TWO

Aloysius, jaunty Aloysius,
Aloysius, get a plumber, eh?

Four Immensely Moral Tales

I. *That We Have Some Delusions of Which it is not Wise to Divest Us*

The jungle night was dark, cold, damp;
Three monkeys, tails curled tight with cramp,
Teeth chittering, huddled on a bough.
"O for one spark of fire, now,"
Sighed one, "to build a blustery blaze,"
And just then glimpsed, to his amaze-
ment, sailing through pit-dark
(What luck, what luck!) just such a spark,
Leapt, caught it, kept it in cupped paws;
The others instantly heaped straws,
Twigs, sticks; all puffed, all blew,
At once in imagination knew
The blessings of a boisterous fire;
Phantasmal flames streaked higher and higher
And all grew warm until, alas!
A great snake reared up from the grass.
"What idiots," sneered the snake, "to try
To kindle fire from a fire-fly!"
The monkeys, as he looped away,
Blinked at each other in dismay,
Then clambered stiffly, clumsily,
Back to their bough, their misery.

Lord! What fools these monkeys be!

II. *That Everything is a Matter of Circumstance*

One day a famous hunter who
Trapped animals for many a zoo
Felt underfoot some branches snap
And fell in his own tiger-trap.
In vain he uttered shriek and shout;
None of his helpers were about
(They having seized the opportunity
To seize his equipment with impunity.)
He sat upon the ground, aghast
To see his Future turn to Past
(But while it still was Future, it
Looked strangely like a tiger-pit.)
In frenzy, then, he vainly tried
To scramble up one or t'other side . . .
At last, being disinclined to starve, he
Dined on a dozen grubs and larvae.
The second week an ape peered in,
Saw him, and began to grin,
Doubtless interpreting his frantic
Caperings as a cunning antic;
Teased him with branches and lianas,
Tossed him (slightly used) bananas
(Which he immediately downed.)
Soon other animals gathered round,
As many as might disembark
From a modern Noah's Ark,
Crowded about on the pit-brim
Expectantly observing him
And *lunched*—but threw him never a bit
Unless he did a trick for it.

The truth burst on him like a storm:
If he would eat, he must perform;
Unless he swallowed down his pride
He would not swallow much beside.
Whereupon he, being mad for food,
Did absolutely all he could:
Walked about upon his hands,
Did somersaults, cartwheels, and headstands,
Recited all the allegations
Brought before the United Nations,
All the Papal dispensations,
Mallarmé (his *Divagations*)
And the seventh chapter of *Galatians*,
Sang the Goldberg Variations
(It's difficult beyond all words
—Try it some time—to sing chords);
Did his inmost and his utmost,
Brain-most, lung-most, in fact gut-most;
Eschewing human dignity,
He strove with all his soul to be
The animals' one-animal zoo;
Do not sneer; for so would you.

III.   *That Nothing is Evidence to Those*
       to Whom it is not Evident

An elephant (reputed wise)
Would not believe in butterflies.
Every effort at persuasion
He met with Johnsonian refutation,
Commencing with a fierce "Har-rumph!"
And ending with a scornful "Humph!"
"Such tales are lies—at best, mistakes.
These photographs?—transparent fakes!
That's all outrageously irrelevant;
If not, declare me not an elephant.
Truths may be proved, most certainly;
Since this is *false,* how can it be?
Sirs, I keep an open mind,
I welcome facts of every kind.
A mountain smaller than a gnat
—There is *some* evidence for that;
We have good reason to suppose
There is a snake with twenty toes;
A fish that starves unless fire is fed it
—Things of that sort I can credit;
But *BUTTERflies*! What utter stuff!
Enough, enough, enough, ENOUGH!
Sirs—you believe that *butter* flies?
Well, then—no more of butterflies!"

One day, as (lecturing his companions)
He strolled beneath baobabs and banyans,
Something chanced to flutter by
—An *indubitable butterfly*!
All watched it as it flitted round
And delicately came to ground.
Our hero roared, "Preposterous!"
Stamped on it—"I refute it thus!
And thus! And thus! And THUS, my friends!"
And snorted loudly at both ends.

(They say he subsequently died,
Whether from rage or wounded pride,
On hearing that a cat in France
Did not believe in elephants.)

IV.   *That if Clothes Make the Man
        it is Dangerous to Undress*

Monsieur Chameau a *boulevardier*
Much too fond of fine array
Woke with a wildly aching head
On hearing footsteps near his bed
And was not greatly comforted
Anon to learn that the said sound
Came from his shoes which walked around
Much as if monsieur *lui-même*
Had been motivating them
Nor felt he happier effect
When his trousers stood erect
And shuffled off to join his shoes
And coat like an ungainly bird
With flapping sleeves took off and soared
(His shirt also) while spats and gloves
Fluttered more delicately like doves
And *pince-nez* and bright bow tie
Played dragonfly and butterfly
Till suddenly these errant clothes
And other articles assembled
Into a figure which resembled
Uncannily Monsieur Chameau
Whereupon and pausing no
Longer than it took to pick
Up *porte-feuille* hat stick
Keys and *carte d'identité*
And pluck from plant in *jardinière*
A most tasteful *boutonnière*
And deeply bow (the while monsieur
Swore not uttering *Sacrebleu*
Nor *Sacre Nom* nor *Nom de Dieu*
But rather many and many a *mot*
Français that you will never know)

This fantasy of clothes although
Empty quite of one Chameau
Strolled most elegantly away
Through the door and down the stair
And out upon the pavement where
The neighbors soon were heard to say
"Bon jour, monsieur" *"Chameau mon cher*
But you surpass yourself today"

Rabbinical Legend

In Paradise before the Fall
Adam was an androgyne;
Towels were embroidered His *and* Hers,
He was his own valentine.

When one was two and two were one,
Who could protest such paradox?
O lovely era when indeed
Love laughed at locksmiths and at locks!

No schism of sexes into sects
Hostile as Ghibelline and Guelf;
Adam wore a constant smile
Of satisfaction with himself.

All creatures, likewise talented,
Felt like contentment with their lot;
No wonder all Creation cried
Marvelling what God had wrought.

Lilith it was who ruined all;
She, in malice or in fun,
Making a triangle of two,
Divorced that happy pair of one.

How wretched was poor Adam then,
When she must see, in helpless woe,
Himself unfaithful to herself,
Her alter ego altered so.

What if such foul sophistic sport
Devised on purpose to perplex
Compounded Trinity to two?
God sighed, and made divided sex.

Knight, with Umbrella

The difficulty with all
Forms of heroism
Is that they require
Appropriate occasions
And that these are rarer
Even than heroes.
Consequently, the hero
Waits and waits,
Exquisitely aware
Of the absence of any
Heroic way
To mail a letter,
Buy theater tickets,
Or put on rubbers.

Most remarkable about
The older heroes
Is their luck in encountering
Punctual dragons
Compliantly belligerent
And maidens regularly
Requiring rescue.
I observe all this
A little bitterly,
Shivering
In rented armor
On an icy corner,
Late for the costume
Party, and reflecting
How long one waits
These days
Even for a cab.

Abdication of the Clown

Here, take the old suit
Of spots and ruffles,
I've only been wearing it
As pajamas
And somehow lately
I just can't sleep.

Take the hat, too.
It's really only
A duked-up dunce-cap
But it's part of the uniform.
And here's the mask:
Take it, you need it

To give you character.
Go on, get in there
And do what they tell you
And hurry, hurry:
The stands are empty,
Everyone else
Is clowning already.

Don't worry about me.
I'll sit right here
Dressed in my skin,
Disguised as myself
And from here on in
I'm only a spectator
Who can't bear to look.

THREE

Hush, fool,
You too have your part in the play.
Play it in ignorance, as fools do.

THE ABSTRACT TRAGEDY

A Comedy of Masks

I'll have these players
Play something like the murder of my father—

Characters

PIERROT
POLICHINELLE
HARLEQUIN
PANTALOON
COLUMBINE

PIERROT *is a mild little man with dark, brilliant eyes set in a pinched, infantile face. He wears a white smock with long loose sleeves, frilled at the wrists; a great cartwheel ruff as collar; loose white trousers; a black skullcap. His face is whitened with flour, and he wears spectacles.*

POLICHINELLE *has "a figure like a bundle of wash"; he wears a seventeenth-century doublet with a frill, and humps in front and back; a black half-mask, a huge red cardboard nose. His costume is black and white. He is small-featured and very fat; at times he quivers with eagerness.*

HARLEQUIN'S *costume is ragged and patched in all colors; he wears a close-fitting jacket and parti-colored tights. His leather girdle has a lath sword stuck in it, and a net containing three small black boxes is tied to it. His head is covered with a wide-brimmed soft black hat with a rabbit's tail in it; when the hat is removed, it discloses his shaved head. He wears a sooty black small mask, like a raccoon's. He has a hatchet-face and a lean, lanky figure. He is always a disturbing person; at times sardonic, at times sinister, at other times sullen; he should never give the impression of being perfectly sane. He has the habit of making menacing gestures with his sword when excited.*

PANTALOON *is tall and thin—with, however, a paunch. He wears a tight-fitting suit of scarlet, with breeches and long stockings of scarlet; a loose red cap; red Turkish slippers, turned up at the toes. Over his suit he wears a long brown bed-gown, or alderman's gown, trimmed with fur; when reversed, this reveals a crimson lining, and so resembles a king's robe. At his girdle he wears a purse which, turned inside out, reveals gold ribbing and velvet lining, so that it resembles a crown. He also wears a very long false nose, which Harlequin gives him as a scepter. He has a pointed gray beard.*

COLUMBINE *is a handsome, healthy, sensual country-wench, of the milk-maid sort; in fact she carries a milk-maid's bonnet. She is blond; she wears a striped gown of green and blue.*

These characters are supposed to be, not the conventional characters of the comedy of masks, nor the abstractions written about by Verlaine, Dowson, and others, but a group of actors who have played the set roles until they have identified themselves with them. The traditional names and costumes should therefore never be allowed to obscure the fact that these are real people, living a hand-to-mouth existence while practicing their profession obscurely in one small town after another.

The time is the late eighteenth century, shortly before the French Revolution.

The place: the stable-loft of an inn in a small town of the Loire valley. The only access to the loft is by ladder and through an open trapdoor. The loft alone is seen. There should be a half-partition behind which Columbine is supposedly sleeping; I suggest that she actually enter, unseen by the audience, at the point of her supposed wakening, so as to avoid a long period of inactivity on the stage.

The loft contains stacked bundles of hay; straw is scattered about its floor. Harness is hung on the walls; there are two small windows, well-veiled in spiderwebs, at the rear of the stage. There are two or three milking-stools, used as seats; an overturned wooden tub serves as card-table. Harlequin's boxes are laid here.

The time of performance is precisely the time of the represented action; that action is continuous, but it may be interrupted, for the convenience of the audience, at whatever point or points the director may desire.

The verse is to be read naturally; *not scanned, nor pronounced with extreme consciousness that it is verse. The actor should not suppose that because a speech is printed as a unit, it must be rattled off as a unit. Study of the speeches will make clear that many of them involve hesitations, false starts, changes of mind, changes of mood, etc.; all of which should be clearly indicated in performance.*

PIERROT: Spades.
POLICHINELLE: *Spades?* What do you mean?
You *haven't* any spades—let me see!
Just as I thought—nothing but clubs!
Clubs, man, *clubs.*
You're impossible, Pierrot;
It's maddening to play cards with you.
Taking clubs for spades—with your spectacles on!
You're blind as a—
PIERROT: Yes. Yes. I know.
I know. I know. I'm going blind.

POLICHINELLE: Oh, no—I didn't mean that at all!

PIERROT: It's all right. It's perfectly true.

POLICHINELLE: What I meant is, you weren't paying attention . . .
Why, you see as well as anyone,
Lots of people take clubs for spades—

PIERROT: It's all right, I said. It's true.
And—you know—it doesn't matter to me.
It's not—the world—that I want to see.

POLICHINELLE: I could bite out my tongue . . . I wouldn't have said it
If I weren't driven half out of my wits
By this rain, this rain—and *her,* over there—

PIERROT: Her?

POLICHINELLE: Her.

PIERROT: She's asleep,
She isn't bothering you.

POLICHINELLE: Isn't bothering me!
I just can't get her out of my mind
It's like a tune that keeps running in my head—

PIERROT: You'd *better* get her out of your mind.

POLICHINELLE: I can't. I can't. Shall we play some more?

PIERROT: No.

POLICHINELLE: Come on—just one more game.

PIERROT: Not now. I'm not in the mood for it.

POLICHINELLE: I'm not either, to tell you the truth.
Well—you owe me twenty million.
Too bad it's only bits of straw.
My God, what rain! Listen to it.
We might as well be under a waterfall.
Something must have sucked up the ocean
And is spewing the whole thing out at once.
You wouldn't think, after nine days,
There'd be that much left up there.

PIERROT: Nine days!

POLICHINELLE: Not to forget our special rain-cloud
That followed us down the whole river-valley
A solid three weeks.

PIERROT: Forget, he says,
Forget—the way Noah forgot the Flood.

POLICHINELLE: ——When was the last time that we played?

PIERROT: How good do you think my memory is?

POLICHINELLE: No, seriously—seriously:
St. Matthew's Day—wasn't it?

PIERROT: What if it was?

POLICHINELLE: Thirty-six days, then!
Thirty-six days—one performance

In thirty-six days!

PIERROT: Well?

POLICHINELLE: Well!

Well—how much did we take in?

PIERROT: How should I know?

POLICHINELLE: That's right;

Not enough to be worth remembering;

And rent for the market-place; lamp-oil; candles;

Grass for the horses; grease for the carts;

Keep for the company at the inn—

PIERROT: So?

POLICHINELLE: So—what are we living on?

PIERROT: Rain.

POLICHINELLE: Rain. What were we paid in?

PIERROT: Rain.

POLICHINELLE: Rain. Can't we get away from it—

Rain, rain—even in talk?

Listen—it's like rivers of dried peas

Pouring onto a thousand drums,

—Just like rivers of dried peas . . .

PIERROT: Enough of your peas. You make me hungry.

POLICHINELLE: *I* make you hungry! Listen, Pierrot,

None of us has ever been anything else.

Herrings, black bread, rotten cheese,

A little watered wine-squeezings

—Just enough to give you the colic—

That's the most we ever had.

The rest of the time—drink from a ditch,

Tighten your belt, sleep under a hedge.

[*Clock strikes four.*]

Four o'clock. Four o'clock.

Well, that's it. No show today.

You can take your costume off, poor fool,

I say there'll be no show today.

I thought we'd make some money for once,

But not a chance. No show today.

PIERROT: Be quiet—do you want to wake her?

POLICHINELLE: Wake her? Yes, I'd like to wake her,

Wake her the way I'd like to wake her . . .

Little white mare, if I ever mount

Into that satin saddle of yours,

I'll ride you and ride you, all night long.

You'll never have had a better rider.

PIERROT: She's never had anyone at all.

POLICHINELLE: What makes you say that? She's married,
    isn't she?
PIERROT: She's married, and she isn't married.
    Pantaloon told me he's never touched her;
    She's always been too frail and sickly.
POLICHINELLE: God, the man's an utter fool!
    Married to a filly like that,
    Just made to ride—and never touched her?
    I don't believe it.
PIERROT: That's what he says.
POLICHINELLE: I don't believe it. He'd have to be made
    Of something other than flesh and blood.
PIERROT: Nevertheless—that's what he says.
POLICHINELLE: Then he's an idiot—he thinks she's sickly?
PIERROT: That's what he says.
POLICHINELLE: Then he's an ass.
    Look at her hair, it's like ripe wheat,
    It shines, shines. Look at her skin:
    Cream, cream. Look at her arms;
    And my God! that corner of her mouth,
    I could spend a month just kissing it.
    She's sickly?
PIERROT: That's what he says.
POLICHINELLE: Then he's an ass. She tells him that
    So that he won't fumble around her
    Like a drunkard who can't find the door.
    Pretty little invalid,
    I could cure your sickness in a minute.
    All you need is a good massage
    And a couple of dozen warm injections . . .
PIERROT: Punch! Shhh! What if she heard you?
POLICHINELLE: She's asleep, isn't she?
    Or if she's pretending
    She's hearing what she wants to hear,
    Hearing what I want her to hear,
    What I'll tell her sooner or later anyway . . .
    I'll go crazy if I don't have her.
    I caught her bathing the other day,
    Bright water sliding down her breasts,
    It hit me like a punch in the belly,
    I nearly died, I could hardly breathe.
    A man can't stand to suffer like that.
    All I want is a single chance,
    Five minutes alone with her . . .
    Just five minutes . . . Say, Pierrot . . .

31

PIERROT: Well, then, Polichinelle?

POLICHINELLE: Everyone knows you're an excellent fellow ...
Always willing to help a friend ...

PIERROT: Thank you for the compliment.

POLICHINELLE: Take a little walk, why don't you?
It's good for the health.

PIERROT: In this rain?

POLICHINELLE: No, I suppose not, —not in this rain.
—You drank a lot of water this morning.

PIERROT: So I did.

POLICHINELLE: That's bad for the bladder.
The water here is death on the bladder,
You ought to get rid of it.

PIERROT: I have.

POLICHINELLE: I suppose you haven't any urgent business
Somewhere else?

PIERROT: None I can think of.

POLICHINELLE: Then why in hell can't you turn your back
And stick your fingers in your ears
To save the lady a certain embarrassment?

PIERROT: She's not embarrassed, she's asleep.

POLICHINELLE: If she is, she's blushing in her sleep.
All right, by God! you can both be embarrassed—!

PIERROT: Don't be a fool.

POLICHINELLE: Let me alone.

PIERROT: Don't be a fool.

POLICHINELLE: I say, let me alone.

PIERROT: Listen, you idiot—Pantaloon
Will come up any minute—do you hear?
He's talking to the innkeeper!

POLICHINELLE: I don't believe you.

PIERROT: Listen yourself.
I can hear them arguing about something.
Can't you hear him?

POLICHINELLE: Yes—you're right. Yes, you're right. It's Pantaloon.
Another time, then, little filly,
Another time ... but sooner or later.
Not that I worry about Pantaloon,
It's just to save—embarrassment.

PIERROT: Yes: it will save embarrassment.

POLICHINELLE: Not that I worry about Pantaloon.

PIERROT: Of course not. But of course you worry.

POLICHINELLE: Of course I do. But not about him.

PIERROT: Naturally.

POLICHINELLE: Naturally.

It's someone else who worries me.

PIERROT: Harlequin.

POLICHINELLE: Yes: that Harlequin.
I don't know what it is, exactly;
It's nothing you can put your finger on;
It's just—*something*.

PIERROT: I know what you mean.

POLICHINELLE: He turns up suddenly out of nowhere,
Somehow becomes our Harlequin . . .

PIERROT: Well, he's a good one.

POLICHINELLE: So he is;
But half the time he goes about
Staring like a sleep-walker
And hearing nothing; or lies around
Slack-muscled as a winter snake,
Playing with those three black boxes,
Three small black boxes in a net.
What do you think he has in those boxes?
Or sharpening that sword of his . . .
Why does he sharpen and sharpen that sword?

PIERROT: I don't know. Why not ask him?

POLICHINELLE: —The rest of the time, he's all energy,
And full of melancholy glee
At some nasty secret joke.
A madman's joke. Do you think he *is* mad?

PIERROT: I don't know. All I know
Is what the innkeeper said about him.

POLICHINELLE: What did he say?

PIERROT: He thought he knew him.

POLICHINELLE: Who is he, then?

PIERROT: He doesn't know.

POLICHINELLE: Doesn't know!

PIERROT: The innkeeper
Thought he was the acrobat—

POLICHINELLE: The acrobat! What acrobat?

PIERROT: One of a wandering troupe of tumblers
Who came through here two years ago.

POLICHINELLE: Well, what of it?

PIERROT: Something happened.

POLICHINELLE: What?

PIERROT: A kind of a tragedy.
He had a woman with him then,
They worked up on the high trapeze.
You know, she swung, he had to catch her.

POLICHINELLE: And he didn't?

PIERROT: And he didn't.

POLICHINELLE: Deliberately?

PIERROT: The innkeeper says
Most people thought, deliberately.
Of course it's impossible to prove
And the police take little interest
When the victim is an acrobat
Or—you know—a strolling player.
Besides, the man—just disappeared.

POLICHINELLE: The swine—to kill a woman like that!

PIERROT: Oh, she wasn't *killed*.

POLICHINELLE: She wasn't?

PIERROT: No.

POLICHINELLE: Crippled horribly, then, crippled
For the rest of her life—

PIERROT: No, she wasn't;
She fell into a hay-cart.

POLICHINELLE: Hay-cart!
She wasn't injured, then, at all?

PIERROT: Not a scratch.

POLICHINELLE: Not even a scratch?
The devil take silly tales like that!
That's trash for old women to pick over.
What does it matter if nothing happened?

PIERROT: Excuse me, Polichinelle:
You miss the point.

POLICHINELLE: What is the point?

PIERROT: The point is not what happened to happen,
The point is what he *meant* to happen.
The point is not that Providence
Had the power to foil a dreadful plan;
The point is that a certain man
Was capable of such a plan.

POLICHINELLE: You're right. I never thought of that . . .
And so the baffled beast slunk off—!
Nevertheless, he stands convicted—

PIERROT: Not convicted—just suspected.

POLICHINELLE: Convicted, I insist, convicted.
Suspected is too good for him . . .
I wish I'd been the judge at his trial.

PIERROT: But there wasn't any trial.

POLICHINELLE: It doesn't matter. There should have been.
I'd have made a tremendous Judge.
I'd have frowned a long while over my books,
Then raised my head and glowered at him.

34

"Harlequin," I would have said,
"That is your full name, Harlequin?
Harlequin, you stand convicted
Of arson, incest, counterfeiting,
Burglary, piracy, horse-stealing,
Swindling, chicken-thieving, poaching,
Sodomy, false impersonation—"
PIERROT: But he didn't *do* any of those things!
POLICHINELLE: It doesn't matter. He's capable of them.
PIERROT: But—
POLICHINELLE: Do you think the Law is a fool, to lock
The barn door after the horse is stolen?
Besides—is it right to let him commit them?
Is the Law an accessory to the fact?
PIERROT: You have a point there.
POLICHINELLE: A point, indeed!
Be quiet, and stop obstructing justice.
Let us proceed. —"Now, then, Harlequin,
Though these are somewhat serious crimes
We might in mercy overlook them
Were it not for the heinous felony
Of seeking to destroy, murder,
Eradicate, and kill—a woman;
A woman, a woman, Harlequin;
A wondrous rose and ivory creature
With eyes reflecting Cupid's fires;
Rose-petal lips; a delicate head
Framed in a fragrant cloud of hair;
And breasts like cups of alabaster
And limbs marvellously smooth;
A dainty Eden of delight—"
PIERROT: Aren't you getting carried away?
POLICHINELLE: Perhaps, a little. "Now, then, Harlequin,
Could you think of nothing better to do
With such an exquisite being as that
Than kill her—kill her? —Answer me,
Wasteful, *wasteful* Harlequin,
Most infamous rascal Harlequin,
Utterly corrupt Harlequin,
Sum of all vices, Harlequin,
—Look up, you hangdog Harlequin,
Look up, look me in the eye
—Do you hear me, pig of a Harlequin?
Answer me—do you hear?"
PIERROT: *Pssst!*

POLICHINELLE: "Answer me, you scoundrel!"
PIERROT: *Pssst!*

[*Enter* HARLEQUIN.]

POLICHINELLE: Huh? Oh—hello, Harlequin.
  We were just—rehearsing a play.
  A really rather remarkable play . . .
  With a fairly fine part for you . . .
  Except that . . . the play is rather poor;
  And the part itself is extremely small . . .
  In fact, you have nothing to say at all
  And nothing to do but get yourself hanged—
  Off-stage—without ever appearing . . .
  You play a vicious criminal,
  An especially odious kind of monster
  Which is—naturally—unsympathetic
  And—naturally—out of character.
  On second thought, you're not even in it,
  It's somebody else of the same name.
  In fact—in fact—
PIERROT: Polichinelle!
POLICHINELLE: To tell you the truth—
PIERROT: Polichinelle!
POLICHINELLE: What the devil do you want?
PIERROT: You're beating your brains out for nothing.
POLICHINELLE: Eh? Eh?
PIERROT: Can't you see?
  He hasn't heard a word you've said.
POLICHINELLE: Not a word?
PIERROT: Not a single word.
POLICHINELLE: You're sure of that?
PIERROT: Absolutely.
POLICHINELLE: Absolutely?
PIERROT: Absolutely.
  He's in one of those odd fits of his,
  He might be a thousand miles away.
POLICHINELLE: Hmmm! Let's test him. —Harlequin,
  You have just inherited a fortune.
PIERROT: See what I mean? He doesn't hear.
POLICHINELLE: Remarkable, remarkable;
  Let's try him further. —Harlequin:
  A beautiful woman was asking for you:
  A great lady, a queen, a duchess
  In a gold coach drawn by silver horses . . .
  A woman like the Queen of Love
  With white breasts like two drifting swans,

A mouth like an opening crimson flower
And thighs, thighs marble-smooth—
PIERROT: You're getting carried away again.
POLICHINELLE: All right, I won't . . .
    She was in tears because she loves you . . .
    She left this purse of golden coins . . .
PIERROT: See what I mean?
POLICHINELLE: It's unbelievable.
    Let's try again. —Harlequin!
    Why are you sharpening that sword?
    Are you trying to make it like your nose,
    Needle-Nose? Are you a man
    Or a gargoyle, Harlequin?
    I've seen prettier things than you
    Carved on a stone gutter-spout.
    You have a face like a rusty hatchet,
    Ears like bats' wings, and snakes' eyes—
    [HARLEQUIN *gives him a sharp whack on the head with his sword.*]
    Ow! —I think he heard me then.
PIERROT: It would seem that he hears certain things,
    Not others; or his fit has left him.
    Both hypotheses fit the facts.
    Continue the experiment.
POLICHINELLE: You continue it, my boy.
    I'm not curious any more.
    [*to* HARLEQUIN] Go on, sharpen that silly thing,
    Sharpen it till there's nothing left of it.
    [*to* PIERROT] Let's play cards.
PIERROT: If you want to.
POLICHINELLE: There's nothing else that we can do.
    Listen to that rain—listen to it!
                   [*They begin play.*]
    Hearts; yes; I'll say, Hearts.
PIERROT: Surely a poet somewhere, some day,
    Will make a poem about the rain,
    —The melancholy autumn rain—
    As melancholy as the rain . . .
    I once heard a blind beggar sing
    A song like that: he and the rain
    Sang it together.
POLICHINELLE: Well, well.
PIERROT: It made me think of the strange music
    Of that ghostly bacchanal
    A whole city heard at night
    When the god of great Antony withdrew,

Deserting him . . .

POLICHINELLE: Give me a card.

PIERROT: The leaves are down; carnival's end:
Masks and confetti underfoot;
Everything trodden into the mud.
—Do you know what an old priest once told me
Carnival meant?

POLICHINELLE: I can't imagine.

PIERROT: He said it was Latin, and it meant
The farewell of the flesh; farewell
Of flesh to all its fleshly joys.

POLICHINELLE: Hmmm? Let's tell 'em hello first;
Farewells come later.

PIERROT: O Polichinelle!
Everything passes—

POLICHINELLE: Well, *I* pass.

PIERROT: Everything passes—What if we die,
Die without ever having lived?

POLICHINELLE: Oh, for the love of God, Pierrot!
I'd rather have a bellyache
Than listen—I don't know which is worse,
You or this God-forgotten rain!
Farewell, hello; hello, farewell;
                    [*Enter* PANTALOON.]
Farewell— Oh, hello, Pantaloon!

PANTALOON: *Hello,* he says. *Hello,* indeed!

POLICHINELLE: Why, what's the matter with *hello?*

PANTALOON: Matter? Matter? Doom's the matter:

POLICHINELLE: Oh, no! You, too?

PANTALOON: Doom, death, bankruptcy, fire, plague,
Famine, and slavery—that's the matter;
And all that *you* say is "Hello!"
Now do you know what's the matter?

POLICHINELLE: No.

PANTALOON: The great tree full of singing birds
Has been put to the axe; the golden strings
Are ravished from Apollo's lyre;
Sealed is the Pierian spring;
Thalia's nightingales are still;
Mute, now, is Melpomene.

POLICHINELLE: Oh.

PANTALOON: You understand that, do you?

POLICHINELLE: Sure—You should have said so in the first place.

PANTALOON: Idiot!

PIERROT: Frankly, Pantaloon,

You could be clearer.

PANTALOON: All right;
All right; I'll make it clearer.
We've been staying at this inn
Over a week—is that clear?

PIERROT: That is clear.

PANTALOON: And it's rained,
Rained, and rained—is that clear?

PIERROT: Quite clear.

PANTALOON: And since it rained,
We could not play. Is that clear?

PIERROT: Very clear.

PANTALOON: And since we couldn't
We've made no money. —Still clear?

PIERROT: Clear indeed.

PANTALOON: And we came here
Without one sou—because it rained
And rained and rained wherever we went
And consequently we could not play
And consequently made no money
And yet spent money all the time.
How about that—is that clear?

PIERROT: Clear as clear.

PANTALOON: Well, then:
That scoundrel of an innkeeper
Claims we owe him forty livres—

PIERROT: Forty livres?

PANTALOON: Forty livres;
And he's holding everything as bond
—Horses, carts, bag and baggage;
Absolutely everything.

PIERROT: Everything?

PANTALOON: Everything.

PIERROT: Scenery too?

PANTALOON: Scenery too.

PIERROT: And stage-lumber?

PANTALOON: Stage-lumber too.

PIERROT: Everything?

PANTALOON: Everything.

PIERROT: But we can't play
Without those things—how can we play
Without those things? If we can't play,
How can we pay?

POLICHINELLE: That's right—how can we pay
If we can't play?

PANTALOON: How, indeed?
I tried to get him to listen to reason;
It's no use.
PIERROT: What'll we do?
What in the world are we going to do?
It's a trap.
PANTALOON: It *is* a trap.
PIERROT: We can sit and listen to the rain.
We can sit here in the rotten straw
Of the stable-loft of an old inn
And listen to the stable rats
Rustling in the rotten straw
And rot ourselves until they come
To throw us into prison-straw
To listen to the prison-rats
And rot there with the rotting straw.
There'll never be another show.
Well—I'll go take my costume off.
PANTALOON: And go naked?
PIERROT: And put my clothes on.
PANTALOON: *Your* clothes? You have no clothes.
The innkeeper has your clothes.
PIERROT: Even our clothes?
PANTALOON: Even your clothes.
PIERROT: You mean we can't change out of costume?
PANTALOON: That's right. You *can't* change.
PIERROT: This is what I always feared.
I always feared it. Now it's happened.
PANTALOON: What do you mean?
PIERROT: I mean I knew
Some day I should *be* Pierrot;
Turn into Pierrot entirely;
Be no one, nothing but Pierrot.
My own life has become a sleep
Between the wakings of Pierrot.
I am nothing but a dream,
A dream dreamed by Pierrot.
I have seen my costume all laid out
Ready for me to put it on
—Cap, blouse, pantaloons, and shoes—
All that makes up a Pierrot—
And feared to see it come alive
Without me, and walk away
Abandoning me; for I know
That I am nothing; only a dream;

Pierrot's dream; shadow of a shadow.
PANTALOON: That's wild talk.
PIERROT: Is it—is it?
Do you think your case is any different?
—Which of you can recall his name
—His *real* name? Well? I thought not.
You are Pantaloon and Polichinelle
And Harlequin; I am Pierrot.
We can't remember anything else.
We'll never *be* anything else.
POLICHINELLE: He's right, you know. I had a name once,
Jean, François, Georges, Paul,
Something like that; but I can't remember it.
It's like trying to remember the name
Of my second cousin's grandfather's cat.
I guess I'm only Polichinelle.
PANTALOON: It's not true! It's not true!
Why, I've lived the realest kind of life.
—*Real life,* all my own,
Nothing to do with Pantaloon;
Just myself and Columbine—
PIERROT: You and who?
PANTALOON: Columbine.
PIERROT: What is her real name?
PANTALOON: Her name?
Uh—Columbine.
PIERROT: And who are you?
PANTALOON: I? Hmmm! —Pantaloon . . .
PIERROT: See? See? There you are!
We have given up our selves, our lives,
To become persons of a play,
Fictions moving in a fiction,
Shadows cast in someone's brain;
And we *are* the persons of a play.
I remember when I was small,
When people were mostly legs and feet
And faces were high up in air
I used to sit with my cat and my dog
On a little bench set in the shade
And watch the hens blaze up or darken
As they walked in and out of the light
And my dog heard sounds I couldn't hear
And my cat saw things I couldn't see
And the hawk in heaven and mole in earth
Saw and heard what I could not;

And everything lived in different worlds
And I thought of the thousand thousand worlds
Hidden from me by my own world
And the single World, the true World,
Hidden from all of us under those worlds . . .
POLICHINELLE: The blacksmith's daughter, when I was five,
Caught me up and gave me a kiss
And held me a moment to her breast
And afterward I buried my face
For one moment in her lap;
I remember how warm, how sweet, her thighs were . . .
PANTALOON: In a sun that went down long ago
Someone told me a noble tale
And my heart swelled so, I couldn't speak . . .
PIERROT: I, I thought once I should see
The world of sense melt away
Like winter's snow, discovering,
As melting snows disclose the Spring,
Reality; the true Truth;
The invisible Mover of the stars;
God's Face behind nature's mask;
The flower to be in the seed of Now.
Instead, my sensual eyes grow blind . . .
POLICHINELLE: I could have sighed out my soul
In the tiny garden Adam found
In Eden Garden; the little cave
Grown over with sweet maidenhair . . .
PANTALOON: What is it he's talking about?
PIERROT: Just what he's always talking about.
POLICHINELLE: —That's the sweet Reality.
I never knew it, never knew it.
I must always play the lecherous clown
Who never can satisfy his lust—
PIERROT: I could sit and howl here in the straw;
I feel like the soul of a dead man
Yearning for the body in the grave.
I am dead; I am dead; and I never lived;
I have never known Reality.
PANTALOON: Now that I come to think of it,
I never knew reality, either.
All I remember of myself
—It *is* like a ghost remembering life—
Was that I had true nobility.
PIERROT: True what?
PANTALOON: True nobility.

POLICHINELLE: That's nice.
PANTALOON: True nobility:
  Yes: nobility, I say;
  Nobility in every bone,
  In every sinew! I could have done
  Numberless great and noble things;
  And I did nothing.
    The great *I*
  Cast in the true heroic mold,
  That could have brought the world to heel,
  Made Alps his footstool, clouds his throne
  —That *I* did nothing. Another *I*
  Played Pantaloon, *is* Pantaloon,
  Pantaloon the impotent cuckold,
  Pantaloon the angry father,
  Pantaloon the miserly merchant,
  Pantaloon after Pantaloon.
  O folly and cruelty of Fate,
  To cut pure Parian marble where
  The god-like form of Ajax slept
  —An Ajax? No—a Hercules!—
  Into a hundred grinning clowns.
  Now I sit penniless in the straw
  And think of prison and hear the rain
  —I, I, who could have done
  Numberless great and noble things,
  Had the occasion only offered.
                    [Harlequin *laughs.*]
[*to* HARLEQUIN]—What the devil are you laughing at?
HARLEQUIN: I? At you—and you—and you.
PANTALOON: At *me?*
PIERROT: Me?
POLICHINELLE: *Me?*
HARLEQUIN: At all of you.
PANTALOON: What's so God damned funny about us?
POLICHINELLE: Yes, what's so funny?
HARLEQUIN: Everything.
  You with your desire to know
  The real Reality—the true Truth;
  The secret Face behind the Mask,
  The flower to be in the seed of Now
  —What do you know? Well—what *do* you?
PIERROT: Nothing, Harlequin. Nothing at all.
  You know, I admitted that.
HARLEQUIN: Nothing at all. And you—you

All of an itch with lechery—
Have you found the balm that soothes it?
POLICHINELLE: Not really; you see, I never—
I mean—well, no; no, not really.
HARLEQUIN: Not really. The hot imagination
Full of writhing shapes—like a basket of eels;
Hot thoughts in bed, in the latrine,
A sidelong look at a girl passing
—That's your kind. And you—you
With all that great, great nobility
Of an Ajax—no, a Hercules:
Tell us what the innkeeper said.
Go on, tell us.
PANTALOON: What did he say?
HARLEQUIN: Yes, what did he say?
PANTALOON: I told you everything.
HARLEQUIN: Everything?
PANTALOON: Everything that mattered:
That we owed him forty livres
And he was holding our possessions
Until we paid him.
HARLEQUIN: And what else?
What else—that *didn't* matter?
PANTALOON: Nothing else.
HARLEQUIN: Nothing else?
I happened to be standing near
And happened to hear you. Shall *I* tell them?
PANTALOON: It is true—he made a certain proposal.
HARLEQUIN: Exactly what *sort* of proposal?
PANTALOON: An impossible proposal.
HARLEQUIN: Impossible? Impossible how?
PANTALOON: It was—in a word—indecent.
HARLEQUIN: Indecent how?
PANTALOON: It concerned—my wife.
HARLEQUIN: Concerned her how?
PANTALOON: I won't say.
HARLEQUIN: Shall *I* say?
PANTALOON: No, no . . . in brief,
He offered to let us use our goods
Until—until we could repay him
If I would let him—use my wife.
POLICHINELLE: Your *wife!*
PIERROT: *Your* wife?
HARLEQUIN: [*to* POLICHINELLE *and* PIERROT] You two be silent!
And your response?

44

PANTALOON: I was indignant.
I said she was a virtuous woman
—Very virtuous—in fact,
Through reasons of health—and my forbearance—
That she was still intact: a virgin;
And what he asked—was impossible.

HARLEQUIN: And *he* said?

PANTALOON: He then offered,
Providing what I said was true,
To cut our bill to twenty livres.

HARLEQUIN: And your response?

PANTALOON: I was indignant.

HARLEQUIN: And he?

PANTALOON: He offered to cancel the debt.

HARLEQUIN: And you?

PANTALOON: I said I would think it over
(Merely to gain time, of course.)

HARLEQUIN: Is that what you said?

PANTALOON: Yes, it was.

HARLEQUIN: Shall I say what you said?

PANTALOON: That is what I said.

HARLEQUIN: You said it was really up to her—

PANTALOON: That's a lie—a dirty lie!

HARLEQUIN: You said it was really up to her
—*Up to her*—and he agreed
And offered you a skin of wine
If you would put the question to her;
And you agreed.

PANTALOON: Another lie!

HARLEQUIN: Is it—is it? And what's more,
Both of you had a glass of wine
Then and there, to bind the bargain.

PANTALOON: One more lie.

HARLEQUIN: A lie, is it?
Wine—there's wine on your breath!
You had plenty of it—by your breath!
Here, you two—come and smell it!
You'll find out if it's a lie!

PANTALOON: It is true I had some wine.
I paid for it.

HARLEQUIN: Paid with what?

PANTALOON: With money, of course.

HARLEQUIN: You had no money.
You turned your pockets out this morning
And they were empty.

PANTALOON: I know—I found it.
    Doesn't anyone believe me?
    I found it in the stable-yard;
    Only a sou . . .
            All right,
    All right, I admit it;
    But I did it only to gain time
    And keep the lot of you out of jail.
    —Don't you believe me? Doesn't anyone?
    —Pierrot? —Polichinelle?
    —*Pierrot?!*
HARLEQUIN: Where is the wineskin?
PANTALOON: I was supposed to get that later.
HARLEQUIN: I saw him give it to you.
PANTALOON: Yes;
    But he changed his mind, he took it back.
    Listen, friends—*please* listen—
    There's some truth in what he says
    And yet—and yet—please listen to me!
    You all know I love Columbine;
    You know how I love Columbine;
    I never touched her littlest finger
    Because of the rare love I bore her
    —She was so frail I might have hurt her.
    I swear she's pure as the day I met her.
    And yet—my friends—I love you, too . . .
    Our situation is desperate,
    I just don't know what way to turn;
    We're out of cash, deep in debt,
    Prison stares us in the face;
    And no way out, nothing to do
    But that one dreadful thing; yes, friends,
    Out of the love I have for you
    I would have sacrificed myself
    And her; she willing, of course; only
    If she were willing; but I know
    You are her heart's blood, as mine,
    She would not see her friends in prison;
    No—it might have meant her death
    But she would have sacrificed herself
    For you, dear friends—
PIERROT and
POLICHINELLE: O Pantaloon!
    Generous, noble Pantaloon!
PANTALOON: Thank you, thank you for those tears,

My dearest friends; poor as I am,
I can only repay you with my own;
See—I give back tear for tear.
Come, Pierrot—wise old friend—
Embrace me; kind, kind Polichinelle,
Help me, support me; I am weak
With my emotion. Ah, ah,
What would life be without friends,
Without true friends? Harlequin,
Do not think ill of me; I know
You *do* think ill, with seeming cause,
With seeming just cause; and forgive you.
Forgive me for my seeming fault
As I forgive you; it is virtue,
It is virtue in you that condemns me;
I esteem that virtue, even though
In this instance you were wrong.
Forgive me; I am a poor old man
Whose only weakness is his love
For his sick wife and his few friends;
And who has but little more to live.
Thank you, thank you, dearest friends . . .

PIERROT and
POLICHINELLE: O forgive him, Harlequin!
Yes, yes: forgive him, Harlequin!

HARLEQUIN: Stop it! Do you hear me? Stop it!
You dolts, you ass-eared idiots—fools!
Can't you see what's under your nose?
This hypocritical old fox
Is making monkeys out of you!

PIERROT and
POLICHINELLE: Shame!
Shame, Harlequin!

HARLEQUIN: Stop it— will you listen to me?
Listen to me: now, then; now, then:
Who's the owner of this company,
Owner, manager, and head,
The one who rakes in all the profits?
You? —Me? —Or Pantaloon?

PANTALOON: Friends, I beg you—

HARLEQUIN: Shut your mouth.
Now, then: who is responsible
In law for all the debts run up?
The owner? Or the hired help?
Anyone knows *that;* the owner.

Now, then, who is liable
To imprisonment for debt?
The owner? Or the hired help?
The owner! Right? Well, then, you fools,
How could you possibly be imprisoned
For *his* debts? And if you can't,
Where's his noble sacrifice?
What's more, what's more: what's he paid you
Since God knows when? He's in *your* debt;
You're his creditors; you can throw him
Into a prison-cell this minute
If you desire. —Can't you see?
This villainous old hypocrite
Is pimping for that wife of his
—Who, I'll wager, is a slut
Always passed off as a virgin
Just to push her price up—why,
She can be a virgin over and over
Five minutes after spreading her legs,
With the help of alum and pigeon's blood!
O fools, fools! He'll sell his wife
To settle with the innkeeper
And cheat us out of our back salaries
And pocket all the profits to come,
Saying it went to settle debts;
Can't you see his plot? Can't you see what he's up to?
POLICHINELLE: Pantaloon—
PANTALOON: Friends—friends!
Please! Please! You wouldn't hurt
Your old friend—friend and benefactor?
HARLEQUIN: Tell the truth—the truth—or I'll throttle you!
PANTALOON: Please—no! —All right,
I confess—I confess!
Only it wasn't a plot at all,
I did it in a moment of weakness . . .
I am a man of high ideals,
—Believe me—of noble aspirations;
Indeed, the noblest I have known;
Only, when it comes to action,
Somehow or other I always weaken
And do something—uncharacteristic.
It's Fate, Fate; my tragic flaw;
It's made the tragedy of my life.
HARLEQUIN: There's your true nobility!
PANTALOON: Forgive me—I must cry.

It is terribly humiliating
To a man of high ideals
And infinite moral sensibility
To have his weakness—his one weakness—
Laid bare, like this, before his friends.
PIERROT and
POLICHINELLE: It is a pitiful thing to see.
  A.pitiful sight. Pitiful!
HARLEQUIN: Bah! You are fools, all of you,
  And he's a rogue; and all of you
  Live on illusions that you are
  —Or could be—better than you are;
  Lament that you play fictions, when
  What you call your real selves,
  Those are the fictions. Each of you
  Is exactly what he wants to be
  And has made himself, and none of you
  Could possibly be anything else.
  You are Pierrot; were born Pierrot,
  Are Pierrot, will die Pierrot.
  You, fool, are Polichinelle;
  And you, you rascal, are Pantaloon.
  And never could be anything else.
PIERROT, POLICHINELLE, and
  PANTALOON: It's a lie!
  It isn't so!
  No, no!
  It isn't true!
HARLEQUIN: *Isn't* it? Well, excuse me;
  I have to go and sharpen my sword.
POLICHINELLE: Why are you always sharpening
  That sword?
HARLEQUIN: Why? Why?
  Because I need some kind of defense
  Against innumerable enemies.
POLICHINELLE: But *that* sword? A *wooden* sword?
HARLEQUIN: A wooden sword's as good as any;
  There is no adequate defense
  Against *my* enemies.
POLICHINELLE: Who are they? Who are these enemies?
HARLEQUIN: Fools, fool.
POLICHINELLE: Fools?
HARLEQUIN: Fools; their name is legion;
  Twenty spring up when one dies;
  They are uniformed in the human shape;

They are cunning; they hide everywhere;
Any face can be an ambush;
But we can tell 'em, my sword and I,
We smell 'em out, we can tell 'em.
POLICHINELLE: How can you tell them?
HARLEQUIN: They always ask me
Why I am sharpening my sword.
POLICHINELLE: And those boxes—those three black boxes—
In that net at your belt—
What are they for?
HARLEQUIN: They're fool-traps, fool,
To trap fools. They'll trap you,
They'll trap you.
PANTALOON: Let him alone,
Let him alone—can't you see he's crazy?
HARLEQUIN: *Crazy!* The battle-cry of fools
Whenever they meet with sense or wit:
Crazy! Crazy! What's not stupidity,
Ignorance, or plain confusion,
That's crazy. Raise the battle-cry!
Oh, it'll be a long war, I tell you!
Eternal war; I won't see the end of it.
POLICHINELLE: Well—why make war on 'em?
What have you got against them, anyway?
HARLEQUIN: What have I got against them—I?
I'll tell you what I've got against them.
All of you have been bellyaching
About your wonderful real selves
And how you lost them in playing clowns
—All crud, of course; you're all just clowns.
But let me tell you about me,
Let me tell you about me:
Do you think I was born to be a Harlequin?
Do you think I'm nothing but a Harlequin?
Listen, I've been an acrobat,
Juggler, magician, lion-tamer,
Rope-walker, wrestler—everything—
You just name it and I've been it
—Everything but one thing:
All but the one essential thing:
The one thing I was born to be.
POLICHINELLE: What's that?
HARLEQUIN: *What's that!*
You'd think anyone could see it;
Fools never do.

POLICHINELLE: Well—what is it?

HARLEQUIN: Here—take a good look at me.

Trouble is, you've never looked.

Take a *good* look, now; look how I'm built;

Look at the expression on my face;

Look at how I carry myself;

Look at the way I walk—see?

Doesn't that mean anything to you?

POLICHINELLE: Well . . .

HARLEQUIN: See? Of course it does.

Anyone who isn't a fool

Or stone blind can see right off,

Fools have to have it pointed out:

I was just born to *help people.*

Yes, sir: born to help people.

POLICHINELLE: To do what?

HARLEQUIN: Help people.

Show 'em how to run their lives.

Arrange things for 'em. Help 'em. Help 'em.

The poor bastards don't have any brains,

Somebody's got to look out for 'em.

POLICHINELLE: I don't know . . .

HARLEQUIN: You don't know!

That's because you're just a fool.

Take the three of you, for instance;

You've all made messes of your lives,

You've admitted it; each of you

Hates what he is and what he does,

Wishes he were somebody else.

A big mess! Take a look

At the people in the inn,

All of 'em hating what they are:

A big mess! Look at the world:

Trouble, trouble everywhere,

War, famine, revolutions:

A big mess! And why? Why?

I could fix the whole thing in a minute;

I've told them that a million times;

Do you think I can get 'em to listen to me?

Not them! It's fools, fools,

It isn't Fate, it's just fools

Kept me from being what I ought to be.

That's why I hate 'em. All right:

They *want* war, they'll *get* war.

POLICHINELLE: How do you know you can—

HARLEQUIN: Can what?

POLICHINELLE: Help them.

PIERROT: Polichinelle!

Let him alone.

HARELQUIN: [*to* PIERROT] Leave *him* alone.

He asked me a question—a fool's question—
But I'm going to answer it. How do I know?
That's a good one. That's rich.
But I'll answer it anyway.
Listen, boy: I *love* people
—Love 'em, see? I want to be good to 'em.
I want 'em to be happy. But who's happy?
So they don't know what's good for them;
I do. It's that simple.

POLICHINELLE: It's simple, all right . . .

HARLEQUIN: Of course it is.

Of course it is. But understand
One thing; one thing:
When I say I love people
I don't mean all those clowns around us:
That's not people, that's fools,
I hate fools. No, sir:
What I love is real people.
You've been talking about your real selves;
That's what I love; the real person
Hidden underneath the fool.
The real person . . . It's hard to get at;
You have to take it by surprise.
You have to take it by surprise,
The real person buried there.
It's like someone buried in a sand-pit,
Trapped in a mine; you have to rescue 'em;
Dig 'em out, or they'll die.
Dig 'em out—then they're happy,
And you're happy because they're happy.

POLICHINELLE: You can make anybody happy?

HARLEQUIN: Of course I can. You for instance;
And you; and you.
I can make you what you want to be.
That's right: what you want to be.
You don't believe me? You don't believe me!
I'll show you—I'll show you!
Wait a minute—wait a minute—
Just a minute now—I've got it!
You want to be a hero—right?

A big hero—like in the tragedies?
Ajax—Hercules? Just name it!
Simple! *You* want to be a seer
Or prophet or something—right? Simple!
And all *you* want—well, we know what you want,
That's the simplest of all.
Simple. As I told you. Simple.
POLICHINELLE: What's so damned simple about it?
  You haven't done anything yet.
HARLEQUIN: Wait a minute—hold your horses!
  We've got to settle something first.
  I want to be sure you clowns are serious.
  I won't do a thing unless you're serious.
POLICHINELLE: Am I serious? Are *you* serious
  Am I serious?! Damn right I'm serious!
HARLEQUIN: Fine. Fine. You're serious.
  You'll be in that garden soon.
  How about you? [*to* PANTALOON]
PANTALOON: I— I—
  Is it—dangerous?
HARLEQUIN: Dangerous? well, now,
  I'm not noble—how should I know?
  The question is—are you serious?
  Do you want to be noble, now, or don't you?
PANTALOON: I— I—
PIERROT: Don't do it, Pantaloon!
  Don't you do it!
PANTALOON: I— I—
HARLEQUIN: All right—don't do it.
  I don't care [*to* POLICHINELLE] All right, you;
  It's all off. Too bad!
POLICHINELLE: No, no! Pantaloon—
  You must do it!
PIERROT: No! Don't!
POLICHINELLE: Think of me, Pantaloon—you've got to!
PIERROT: Don't! There's something fishy about it!
HARLEQUIN: Argue it out, I don't care,
  I'll just sit here and sharpen my sword.
POLICHINELLE: Pantaloon!
PANTALOON: I—don't—know—
  I've always wanted to be heroic,
  I've really always wanted to,
  Except I was afraid to do it.
  I'd really like to be noble
  If I only knew it wasn't dangerous

Or painful or perhaps unhealthy
Or terrifying or expensive
Or strenuous or unpopular
Or illegal or uncomfortable,
I surely would like to be noble . . .
POLICHINELLE: Pantaloon! Please! Please!
PIERROT: Don't you do it, Pantaloon!
POLICHINELLE: Please . . . please . . . please . . .
please . . . ?
PANTALOON: Harlequin—?
HARLEQUIN: Suit yourself.
I don't care. It's nothing to me.
PANTALOON: Harlequin, I— I—
I guess— I guess I'd—like to try.
HARLEQUIN: All right. It's on again.
Look, you're getting noble already;
That was a hero's choice.
PANTALOON: Hmmm!
HARLEQUIN: [to PIERROT] Now, then—how about you?
PIERROT: No. I won't.
HARLEQUIN: That does it,
It's all off.
POLICHINELLE: Pierrot, I beg you!
PIERROT: There's something very funny here.
I won't help you make fools of yourselves.
HARLEQUIN: It's all right. He's scared.
PIERROT: I'm not scared.
HARLEQUIN: Aren't you, though?
—It's just too bad for you fellows;
I could have given you what you wanted;
But he had to go and get scared.
PIERROT: I'm not scared.
HARLEQUIN: Sure. Sure.
I'll bet you're not.
PIERROT: I just don't trust you.
I don't think you can do a thing
But get us into a lot of trouble.
HARLEQUIN: You say I can't do anything
And then won't give me a chance to do it.
Fine thing! Well—I don't care.
Too bad, though, for you fellows.
POLICHINELLE: Pierrot, listen!
PANTALOON: Friend Pierrot,
This is hardly heroic of you.
It's not what I'd call heroic behavior.

POLICHINELLE: Pierrot, for God's sake—!
PIERROT: Oh, be quiet.
                    [*to* HARLEQUIN]
    Tell us first what you plan to do.
HARLEQUIN: Tell you what I plan to do . . .
    Well, isn't that just lovely, now?
    Tell you what I plan to do.
    I told you I'd have to use surprise;
    Where's that—if you know what I plan to do?
    You won't even say you're serious;
    I just tell you what I plan to do.
    Excuse *me*.
POLICHINELLE: Pierrot—you're killing me!
PANTALOON: Pierrot, the man who holds back
    When his heart's desire is within grasp
    Must lose both heart and heart's desire,
    Losing what he feared to venture
    And what with venturing he would gain—
HARLEQUIN: Spoken like a hero.
PIERROT: If I truly thought
    I could catch one glimpse of Reality,
    Of what's to be; how the Power moves
    That rules men's minds—
HARLEQUIN: I can give you that.
POLICHINELLE: Pierrot!
PANTALOON: Pierrot!
PIERROT: Well—I'll do it.
POLICHINELLE: Bravo!
PANTALOON: Bravo!
HARLEQUIN: Another hero.
    All right, then—the game's on.
    All of you are serious.
    I interpret that to mean
    You will do whatever I say,
    Everything I tell you to,
    Just that, and nothing more.
    Promise me that.
POLICHINELLE: I promise!
PANTALOON: Well . . .
HARLEQUIN: Well what?
PANTALOON: I was about to say
    I promise, too.
HARLEQUIN: Good. [*to* PIERROT] And you?
PIERROT: It's against my better judgment.
HARLEQUIN: Oh, come! Are you going to hem and haw

And hesitate all over again?

PIERROT: No. I won't. I promise. There.

POLICHINELLE: Bravo again! Friend Pierrot,
You've never been wiser in your life.

PIERROT: I wish I were sure of that.

POLICHINELLE: [*to* HARLEQUIN] Now what?

HARLEQUIN: For the moment, nothing. I'm reflecting.
[*laughs*]

POLICHINELLE: What are you laughing at?

HARLEQUIN: A joke.
A good joke.
[*laughs again*]

POLICHINELLE: What's that?

HARLEQUIN: That's my business. No—I'll tell you;
It doesn't matter. Just a minute:
I have to laugh again. There:
It's this: you promised what you promised
And I'm holding you to that promise.
Do you realize what that promise means?
It gives me absolute power over you,
Even power of life and death.
Yes, sir; yes, sir:
What I want to happen is going to happen;
What I don't want to happen, won't;
You can forget about God and Fate;
I'm Fate as far as you're concerned;
I'm God as far as you're concerned;
[HARLEQUIN *removes his hat and tosses it into
a corner, as if in token of his changed condition.*]
I couldn't ask anything more than that.
Yes, sir: I'm *It;* and *that's* funny.

PIERROT: And what's so funny about that?

HARLEQUIN: Why, look: here I was helping you
To be whatever you wanted to be
And thinking about nothing but that,
And all of a sudden, here I am,
Doing what I always wanted,
Being what I was born to be.
Odd, isn't it?

PIERROT: *Very* odd.

HARLEQUIN: All right, here we go,
Let's get started. [*to* POLICHINELLE] Give me those cards.

POLICHINELLE: Give you what?

HARLEQUIN: The cards, the cards.

POLICHINELLE: What have cards got to do with it?

HARLEQUIN: Just shut up and hand 'em over.
   I'm going to fix up your case first.
POLICHINELLE: Me!
HARLEQUIN: Quiet—I'm reflecting . . .
   Christ, but cards are stupid things.
   Only a fool would fool with them.
   Imagine a fool fooling around
   With a lot of paper kings and queens
   When he could work with the real thing;
   Make real people do what he wants . . .
   And how could this muck tell your fortune?!
   But you can make it *make* your fortune,
   Yes, sir; yes, sir.
   One way's by gambling; the other way
   Is—I'll show you what it is.
   Come here, now.
      Let's look you over,
   Let's see what kind of a lover you make.
   You'll never get anywhere looking like that;
   Take off your mask—hmmm! Hmmm!
   Now that false nose—well, well!
   Put 'em back on; on second thought
   You look a little better with 'em.
   Yes, they *do* do something for you.
   You should take something for your blood;
   Your face is like a plateful of strawberries.
   And you're too fat—much too fat;
   You've got too few features for your face.
   You really ought to shave closer;
   Still—how can anyone shave pleats?
   Stand up straight—straight, I said.
   Is that straight? —Take this off.
   It won't come off? —My God,
   I swear I thought it was part of your costume.
   How about this? That, too?
   That's just *you?* Unbelievable!
   Your figure's like a bundle of wash!
   Now, are you really standing straight?
   In that case, don't. Now, look amorous;
   No, let's have a languishing look;
   Oh, *no!* No, look stern;
   No, proud; no, impetuous;
   Well, try sad; friendly; timid.
   Well, well, it doesn't matter.
   Women have loved bulls and swans,

This one may be mad about baby whales.
Here, now: pay attention.
See this card? It's your card,
The Knave of Hearts; and this card
Is the Knave of Spades, standing next to you
And telling you what you are to do.
See, see—he carries a sword,
Just like me; and this card
Is the Queen of Hearts; she's asleep
But she may wake, soon, and listen.
She's a beauty, isn't she?
Your Knave of Hearts wants to cover her
But she's guarded by two cards:
The King of Hearts—she's his queen.
My, he's noble—isn't he noble?
Heroic, heroic. This last card
Is the Knave of Clubs; he looks wise,
Doesn't he? But notice this:
There's something the matter with his eyes,
He seems half-blind. That's all,
There you are: five cards,
As many as the people in this room.
Now, the thing you have to do
Is make love—*out loud*—
To the pretty Queen of Hearts
Without her guardians noticing.
Tell her how beautiful she is,
Tell her how you worship her,
And all the pretty things you'll give her,
And how happy you will make her.
Get her to slip outside with you.
Meanwhile this clever man with the sword
Will help you.—Do you understand?
POLICHINELLE: No.
HARLEQUIN: Oh, my God! Think, man, think!
    Just think!
POLICHINELLE: But I—
HARLEQUIN: Be quiet; think;
    This isn't a game; it's for real.
PIERROT: This is utter gibberish.
PANTALOON: Gibberish.
HARLEQUIN: Good, good;
    Hear that? They call it gibberish.
    Now play your cards right: woo, man, woo!
    And next, our hero. Let me see:

This, I take it, is your belly?
A pity it is not your chest,
You would have had a heroic chest.
Still—a kingly figure, kingly;
And not without an heir apparent.
Well, let's *make* you king.
PANTALOON: Me king?
King of what?
HARLEQUIN: A kingly question:
Why, king of yourself: a goodly kingdom,
And more than many a king could rule.
PANTALOON: Nothing but that?
HARLEQUIN: Ambitious king!
Why, man, you are a little world
Watered by rivers in your blood,
Patched of continents of your flesh,
Forested too—a whole world,
Yes, and a populous one, too.
    [*removing a louse from his hair and stamping on it*]
Will you ask more?
PANTALOON: But why am I king?
HARLEQUIN: Because you have chosen to be that;
To choose to be is to become.
Pierrot, let's find him royal robes—
Is a king to wear an alderman's gown
And a burgher's cotton night-cap?
There—
    [*taking off his gown, reversing it, and putting it on him as a mantle*]
robe—
    [*taking his purse, reversing it, and putting it on him as a crown*]
crown—
    [*taking off his false nose and giving it to him as a scepter*]
scepter—
You can lead your subjects by the nose!
Look at him, Pierrot, look at him!
Long live the king! —Polichinelle,
Doesn't he look for all the world
Like your King of Hearts?
POLICHINELLE: King of Hearts?
PIERROT: *This is all foolery, Harlequin—*
HARLEQUIN: Foolery? What is foolery?
PIERROT: —To turn his purse inside out
And call it a crown; to reverse
His coat, and call it royal robes;
To give him his false nose for a scepter—

HARLEQUIN: Stop! Stop! —Are you king or not?
Answer me: are you king?
PANTALOON: I . . . had somewhat the . . . feeling of a king . . .
Just for a moment, of course . . . although—
HARLEQUIN: That's enough. He's a king:
Will you rob him of his kingdom?
PIERROT: But it's not true!
HARLEQUIN: You were the one,
I thought, who could not know what truth was.
Now you claim to know it, do you?
O clown with the face of a dead child
Set in a great wheel of ruff,
You are blinded by those sensual eyes;
What will you see when those strange eyes,
Brilliant as jewels, are jewel-blind?
—Let's find out.
PIERROT: My spectacles!
HARLEQUIN: Your spectacles. And now—snap!
And now—stamp—and stamp again.
There we are!
PIERROT: My spectacles!
Why did you smash them—why?
HARLEQUIN: Because
Now you must see with the soul's eyes
—With the soul's eyes—or not at all.
The seer must be blind to see,
The great Tiresias was blind.
PIERROT: He's mad. Mad—or I am.
HARLEQUIN: That's the beginning of your wisdom.
Wisdom is madness to the ignorant,
All who learn the truth go mad.
Learn and be silent.
    Pantaloon,
You're the very image of a king;
But only the image of a king,
The counterfeit, painted picture only
Unless that picture comes to life
In kingly action.
PANTALOON: What shall I do?
HARLEQUIN: You'll perform a hero's part,
Or rather, all parts of all heroes:
Ajax, Hercules, Oedipus, all,
All rolled in one.
PANTALOON: All in one?
HARLEQUIN: All in one. We'll play a play.

PANTALOON: A play!

PIERROT: A play!

PANTALOON: Only a play?
A mere fiction?

HARLEQUIN: Were you the ones
Lamenting, not an hour ago,
That you had turned your lives to fictions?
That all your action was play-acting?
That you were allotted clowns' parts only?
And will you hem, now, and hang back
—Now that I offer you better parts
You said you were born for?
I have your promise
You would do what I told you; will you go back on it?
If so, you are clowns, clowns indeed;
Clowns, and poorer than before.

PANTALOON: I have had a taste of my own majesty.
Though the tokens of my sovereignty
Are trash, the sovereignty is real.
I have been a king; I will continue.

HARLEQUIN: That's how a king speaks.

PIERROT: He *is* kingly—
He *is* kingly!

HARLEQUIN: And you grow wiser.
Shall we proceed?

PIERROT and PANTALOON: Yes—yes.

HARLEQUIN: I warn you, this play is dangerous:
It is no play; it is no fiction;
Whatever happens will really happen;
Are you with me still?

PANTALOON: Proceed, proceed.

HARLEQUIN: I'll call it—hmmm! I'll call it "Life:
The Universal Tragedy."
And now, O death-mask of a cherub,
I'll tell you all that is to happen:
Here's your knowledge of the Future.
You will see how God and Fate work,
And you must warn our kingship here;
And you, O king, must not believe him;
A prophet must never be believed.
Come here, great Sage; he mustn't hear me.
                              [*whispering*]

PIERROT: What? No! No—you can't!
You mustn't, Harlequin, you mustn't!
Pantaloon! Pantaloon!

PANTALOON: Who calls a king by a clown's name?
   I'll hear nothing of Pantaloon,
   Pantaloon concerns me not.
PIERROT: King, then, king: but listen to me—
PANTALOON: Speak; but I'll follow my own course.
PIERROT: Listen to me; you must stop this;
   Stop this, do you hear? Stop it;
   You've fallen into a madman's trap,
   This man is a lunatic—!
PANTALOON: He is Fate, as he tells me,
   And I believe him; he has made me
   At last what I was fated to be.
   I will be faithful to my fate.
POLICHINELLE: Harlequin! I understand!
   Now I see what you meant:
   He's a king, and here's a king,
   And I—I—
HARLEQUIN: Hush, fool,
   You too have your part in the play.
   Play it in ignorance, as fools do.
POLICHINELLE: I will— I will!
PIERROT: Polichinelle,
   Help me—help!
POLICHINELLE: On with the play;
   I know my part, now!
PIERROT: Then I'll fetch help,
   I'll fetch it!
HARLEQUIN: You'll break your neck;
   Blind as you are, you'll break your neck;
   Keep away from that trap-door.
PIERROT: I'll call for help, then. Help! Help!
HARLEQUIN: The wind and the rain will drown you out.
PANTALOON: Come, man: enough of this;
   You will hardly credit this, Pierrot,
   But a strange thing has happened to me.
   For the first time in my life
   I have had a sense of what I am.
   I no longer need this trash.
         [discarding "robe, crown, and scepter"]
   I am myself; king of myself.
   Play your part; I know mine,
   As king.
PIERROT: King—yes, king.
   Pitiful king of a frail kingdom
   Of nerves and sinews, flesh and bone;

King of ten fingers and ten toes—
PANTALOON: And of my soul, of my own soul.
Do not forget my soul, Pierrot.
PIERROT: Yes, please God, king of your soul.
PANTALOON: What is wisdom's warning?
PIERROT: Doom.
Doom—doom. King and kingdom
Alike are doomed.
PANTALOON: When shall this be?
PIERROT: This very day. This hour. Now.
PANTALOON: By what omens do you know this?
I have heard, when kings and kingdoms die,
The dead walk, heaven and earth forewarn;
What was the warning?
PIERROT: To this kingdom
Comes no warning. The rain fell
And a rat rustled in the straw
But these had nothing to do with you.
A fly died in a spider's web,
A bird sat huddled on a bough,
But these had nothing to do with you.
PANTALOON: From what quarter does doom come?
PIERROT: From your own act.
PANTALOON: How can that be?
PIERROT: You have chosen to make a fatal choice.
PANTALOON: What choice have I made? I know of no choice.
PIERROT: You have chosen already.
PANTALOON: And if I have
A choice remaining, how am I caught?
Free to choose, I still am free.
PIERROT: Choose, and see.
PANTALOON: What shall I choose?
HARLEQUIN: Choose one of these.
[HARLEQUIN *holds out the three small black boxes.*]
PANTALOON: Choose one of these?
POLICHINELLE: Sweet, if night of thy sweet eyes
Holds thee in slumber, may I be
Nightingale of that sweet night—
PANTALOON: What is that fool bawling about?
POLICHINELLE: Or if perchance thy sweetest eyes
Are open, making sweetest day,
May I be lark to that sweet dawn—
PANTALOON: Am I to be caught, like a fly in honey,
With all this sweetness? Stop him, for God's sake!
HARLEQUIN: Move over here, Polichinelle;

Woo adequately, but less loudly.
POLICHINELLE: Good, good, I will. May I be lark
  To that sweet dawn—
PANTALOON: Why must he bawl so
  If doom awaits me?
HARLEQUIN: Because doom awaits you.
  That's the kind of tragic chorus
  The world affords you, in reality:
  It's one of the pleasantries of Fate
  That where disasters congregate
  A fool must stand by and be happy.
  Enough of talking, now. Choose.
PANTALOON: Choose among what?
HARLEQUIN: Fortunes, fortunes.
PANTALOON: How shall I know what I choose?
HARLEQUIN: You cannot.
PANTALOON: What fortunes?
HARLEQUIN: Wealth, power,
  Life, Death: all sorts.
  Choose, choose.
PANTALOON: If I refuse?
HARLEQUIN: Refusal is choice. To refuse is to choose.
PIERROT: King, beware the empty box;
  The empty box; that's death!
POLICHINELLE: I'll give thee everything I have—
PANTALOON: And which is that?
HARLEQUIN: You cannot know.
POLICHINELLE: To be my sweetest, sweetest love—
PANTALOON: I am to be noble still?
HARLEQUIN: If you can.
PANTALOON: How can I be
  With that numskull dinning in my ears?
  I can't think.
HARLEQUIN: That's fated, too:
  One must play his part amid distractions.
POLICHINELLE: I see thou hearest me, my sweet;
  I go; haste thou, on sweet feet.
  —Ta-ta, friends; enjoy the play.
                    [*Exit* POLICHINELLE.]
PANTALOON: All that racket, for one rhyme?
HARLEQUIN: Choose, choose.
PANTALOON: And if I choose
  The empty box—that's death?
HARLEQUIN: That is death.
PANTALOON: Real death?

HARLEQUIN: Real death.

PANTALOON: I choose—I choose—

    [COLUMBINE *wakens; stretches, murmuring sensually.*]

COLUMBINE: Hmmm! Mmmm! Mmmm! Mmmm!

    I've just had the most beautiful dream . . .

    Mmmm! the most beautiful dream!

    Mmmm! the most beautiful dream . . .

PANTALOON: What did you dream?

COLUMBINE: None of your business.

HARLEQUIN: Choose—choose.

COLUMBINE: What's he choosing?

HARLEQUIN: One of three boxes.

COLUMBINE: Well, he'll choose

    The wrong one. Be sure of that.

PIERROT: It's just a play.

COLUMBINE: Plays, plays—

    What's it called?

PIERROT: It's called "Life."

COLUMBINE: Well, it won't go. Be sure of that.

    Somebody else has used the subject.

                   [*a whistle from below*]

PANTALOON: What's that?

COLUMBINE: How should I know?

PANTALOON: Harlequin, this is serious?

    What is happening is really happening?

HARLEQUIN: It is serious. It is really happening.

PANTALOON: If I choose the wrong box, I shall really die?

HARLEQUIN: You will really die.

PANTALOON: Then I refuse.

    That's what I choose. I refuse to choose.

    I won't die for a madman's prank.

HARLEQUIN: Madman's prank or not—refuse

    And you choose dishonor and contempt,

    Ridicule, contumely, disdain;

    Turn back to the low clown you were,

    Play the low part you always played.

PANTALOON: No! No! I won't do that!

    Though I am king of this kingdom only,

    King of ten fingers and ten toes,

    I am king of that.

PIERROT: Pantaloon!

PANTALOON: I know no one of that name.

    Give me the boxes.

        I choose—this.

    The empty one!

65

PIERROT: The empty one!

HARLEQUIN: The empty one.

PANTALOON: Wait—Wait—
Let me see; they're all empty!

HARLEQUIN: All empty.

PANTALOON: It's a trick!

HARLEQUIN: Fate's trick—the illusion of choice
Where there is no choice.

PANTALOON: A mere trick!

HARLEQUIN: A mere trick. Will you withdraw
Because it's a trick? Deny your choice?
Refuse to choose? Be Pantaloon
And live? Live to be Pantaloon?

PANTALOON: If this is mischief, to give madmen
An eerie cause for eerier laughter,
I have nothing else to say.
But if you are in earnest—if
You have indeed become my Fate—
I will tell you, I am in earnest, too.
I have heard of men who went to death
As to their mistress; I could not do that,
I dread the dark dust-bin of the grave,
I dread to lie in darkness there
With rags, bones, bottles, broken things;
I dread it. Yet if to live
Is still to inhabit a refuse heap,
Only to be alive in it,
To crawl it, with other crawling things,
With all my senses telling me only
That I am one more crawling thing
Of things that crawl the refuse heap,
I dread that more; let the grave have me
And shape the elements that made me
To something better.

HARLEQUIN: Withdraw, or die.

PANTALOON: I will not withdraw. I have chosen.
In a blind choice where there was no choice
I still have chosen. You cannot undo that.

HARLEQUIN: Well, I'll withdraw.

PANTALOON: And you cannot;
If you owe me death, pay me; pay me.

COLUMBINE: It'll never, never, never go;
He just isn't convincing enough.
                              [*whistle again*]
I've got to go down for a breath of air.

66

I've just got to get a breath of air.

[*Exit* COLUMBINE.]

HARLEQUIN: Another kind of tragic chorus.
 There must be critics by, to doubt
 The sincerity of your suffering . . .
 Now there's nothing but to die.
 That's all there is to tragedy:
 A noble soul, a bad choice,
 And then the consequence. Speak your speech;
 Your last speech.

PIERROT: Harlequin!

PANTALOON: But why must this happen to me? Why?

HARLEQUIN: So that you should question why.
 Come, your speech:

PANTALOON: If I must die,
 I am truly sorry that since
 My life had meaning only to me
 My death can have meaning to me only.
 For this I am sorry. For nothing else.

HARLEQUIN: Good! And now—

PIERROT: Harlequin—don't!

HARLEQUIN: And now—the element of surprise:
 I said I would take you by surprise.
 You know what I mean by surprise?
 I'll give you an instance. I guess I told you
 I used to be an acrobat.
 A girl was with me in the act.
 We worked up on the high trapeze.
 Well—that girl was wild about me,
 Simply couldn't get enough of me,
 Gave me everything she had,
 Trusted me more than her own hands.
 She knew I would catch her every time
 She swung out and let go—you see?
 Do you think I gave a damn about that?
 About *that?* Not me;
 That was nothing but plain fool.
 What *I* wanted was the real thing.
 So once when she swung, I didn't catch her.
 —Deliberately. Didn't even try.
 I knew what showed then in her face
 When she saw I was just letting her fall,
 That was *her*—the real person—
 The person she'd been hiding from me . . .
 Too bad—too bad I didn't see her.

Somebody let out a scream
And I, like a fool, looked away; missed it.
But I won't miss *your* expression—no!
PANTALOON: What's all this about surprise?
Do what you have to do—get on with it!
HARLEQUIN: In good time—in good time—
[*There is a moment of waiting. Then screams come from below.*]
PANTALOON: What is that?
My God what is it?
HARLEQUIN: That's the surprise. That's the surprise.
[*screams*]
PANTALOON: What is it?
HARLEQUIN: It's Columbine.
PANTALOON: Columbine!
PIERROT: What's the matter?
HARLEQUIN: Stand back—keep back.
Good—he's taken away the ladder,
You can't get down. It's Columbine;
Polichinelle's got hold of her.
All this was a clever trick
To get her away from you—for him.
All a trick, you poor fool;
Not for his sake, no, no,
But to give you a sense of dignity
And then pull out the props from under
And let you fall—to the worse fool
Hidden under the layers of fool.
Back, back to your clownship!
PANTALOON: No!
HARLEQUIN: Yes! Back to your clownship—back!
Shall the dung-beetle quarrel with the dung?
That's the surprise. Ah, ah,
That's what you look like. Ah, ah,
That's what you look like. . . .
Fool, fool, nothing but fool. . . .
PIERROT: You scum! You dirty Harlequin!
You lied to me—you dirty Harlequin!
HARLEQUIN: I'm Fate—Fate's a Harlequin.
Ah, ah.
PANTALOON: No—No!
Pierrot, Pierrot—help me—help me!
I can't bear it! I can't bear it!
PIERROT: [*wresting* HARLEQUIN'S *sword from him and
stabbing* PANTALOON]
Give me that—give me it!

There—there—be at peace.
HARLEQUIN: You've killed him!
PIERROT: Blood—real blood—
   Real blood on a make-believe sword!
HARLEQUIN: You'll hang for this, you'll hang for it,
   They'll hang you for it!
PIERROT: Pantaloon's dead;
   And I'll hang; and be dead too.
   Real blood—on a make-believe sword!
HARLEQUIN: Why did you do it?
PIERROT: He was suffering.
   I couldn't stand to see him suffer.
HARLEQUIN: A clown's act—done upon a clown.
   I was only showing him his true self,
   I was only doing what God and Fate do
   To every one of us, every day.
   Only showing him what he was.
   —A clown's act—done upon a clown!
PIERROT: No. No. If Fate's a Harlequin
   —A dirty Harlequin like you—
   And perhaps it is—we can still beat it.
   You told him he was noble
   And he believed you and was noble;
   His choice was a noble choice, his death
   A noble one; he was noble in spite of you.
HARLEQUIN: It's a lie; there's nothing noble;
   There's nothing but reality—
PIERROT: And reality can be noble.
   I learned that through your dirty trick;
   Reality can be noble.
   I had that knowledge in spite of you,
   In spite of you, in spite of you.
   Reality can still be noble.
   We have beaten you, he and I.
   Beaten you.
HARLEQUIN: No!
PIERROT: Yes! Beaten you!
   Farewell, king; it was a king's death,
   It is possible; *still* possible.
HARLEQUIN: [*mockingly*] The great sun has gone down!
PIERROT: And you
   Must walk in darkness.
   [PIERROT *sinks into a trance of grief and meditation from which*
      HARLEQUIN *endeavors vainly to arouse him in the ensuing.*]
HARLEQUIN: It's too bad,

It means trouble . . . It'll go hard with you.
We could claim it was an accident,
An accident while rehearsing a play . . .
We've got witnesses to prove that . . .
Or we could wait till it's good and dark,
Dump him somewhere in a ditch,
Just know nothing at all about it . . .
That's better . . .

                    [*cries from below*]
What's that?
POLICHINELLE: Help, help!
HARLEQUIN: Who's that?
It sounds a little like Polichinelle
—Polichinelle with his head in a barrel . . .
He sounds as if he were down a well.
Who is it?
POLICHINELLE: Polichinelle.
HARLEQUIN: You don't sound like Polichinelle.
Come, who is it? Don't try to fool us!
POLICHINELLE: Polichinelle, Polichinelle!
HARLEQUIN: You don't even look like Polichinelle
What do you want of us, anyway,
Posing to us as Polichinelle?
POLICHINELLE: Help, help!
HARLEQUIN: Help with what?
POLICHINELLE: Help me—help me with this ladder.
HARLEQUIN: It is—it is Polichinelle.
It can't be. But it is—it is.
Look at him!
[*Enter* POLICHINELLE. *He is in an extremely bedraggled condition.*]
POLICHINELLE: Yes, look at me.
HARLEQUIN: Who would ever have thought it possible?
In twenty minutes—twenty minutes—
She's aged him at least twenty years.
POLICHINELLE: Twenty! Twenty thousand years!
HARLEQUIN: She must be a tigress.
POLICHINELLE: A tigress—yes!
And fifty panthers.
HARLEQUIN: He's half dead.
POLICHINELLE: More than half!
HARLEQUIN: All the life's drained out of him;
No man could deal with a woman like that
Twice and live.
POLICHINELLE: Twice! *Once!*
HARLEQUIN: She may have crippled him for life.

POLICHINELLE: Yes, yes—crippled for life.

HARLEQUIN: Look at him—he can hardly stand.

POLICHINELLE: Oh, oh, I *can't* stand!

[*collapses*]

HARLEQUIN: She's a vampire!

POLICHINELLE: A vampire, *yes!*

HARLEQUIN: Think of this, friend Pierrot—

[PIERROT *pays no attention.*]

    If he dies—as he well may—
    He will have died of his great love.
    It is a very solemn thing.
    We are privileged to witness this:
    A martyr in his martyrdom—

POLICHINELLE: Ah, a martyr—true, true!

HARLEQUIN: This is a very hallowed place.
    One day it may be a shrine.
    A monument may mark this spot,
    Depicting our St. Polichinelle
    Together with two faithful friends
    Who in his last agonies
    Did not desert him. Wait, wait:
    I can just imagine it.
    Here—let me kneel and hold your head;
    So; no, so; how is that?
    Do I look graceful? Perhaps—profile?

POLICHINELLE: Good; but Pierrot isn't in it.

HARLEQUIN: He's shown as absent for a moment
    —Gone for help. How do I look?
    Wait a minute—I'll try to weep.
    —No, just a minute, Polichinelle,
    You throw the whole thing out of balance;
    And the sight of a corpse is too depressing.
    We'll just show me—just me—like this:
    "Harlequin grieving for Polichinelle."
    —Or perhaps simply: "Harlequin grieving."
    I always like a simple inscription.
    There: how does our monument look?

POLICHINELLE: Sublime; sublime.

HARLEQUIN: You think so?
    Myself, I don't think it does me justice.
    —You are fortunate, Polichinelle.

POLICHINELLE: Fortunate? I?

HARLEQUIN: Very fortunate;
    To die in the full gratification—

POLICHINELLE: Gratification? Gratification!

HARLEQUIN: In possession of your heart's desire,
The loved, the exquisite Columbine—
POLICHINELLE: That bitch! That bitch!
Don't you mention her to me!
HARLEQUIN: You don't love her any more?
POLICHINELLE: I wouldn't touch her with a barge-pole!
—You know how much I loved her once,
I would have given her all I had—
HARLEQUIN: How much was that?
POLICHINELLE: No matter—a trifle—
To lovers all such things are trifles—
Well—I was talking nicely to her,
Even with appropriate gestures
When she jammed her knee into my groin
And the innkeeper came out of nowhere
And gave me an awful punch in the jaw
Followed by a tremendous kick
That laid me absolutely flat
And while I was lying helpless there
The two of them—the two of them—
HARLEQUIN: The two of them what?
POLICHINELLE: I just can't—
I just can't bring myself to say it.
HARLEQUIN: Whisper it. The two of them—what?
What? *That?* And that, too?
What—and that?
Oh, this is marvellous,
Marvellous, stupendous, marvellous,
The cream of the jest! You poor fool!
POLICHINELLE: I am a fool.
HARLEQUIN: You poor fool;
Carrying out your silly plan—
POLICHINELLE: *My* plan—*my* plan!
Wait a minute—wait a minute!
Just who are you laughing at, anyway?
I ought to punch you right in the nose,
Punch you right in your needle-nose.
My plan! It was *your* plan—
Your silly, stupid plan—
That's what failed. I got hurt;
I got hurt; but your plan failed.
HARLEQUIN: My plan failed?
POLICHINELLE: You bet it failed.
HARLEQUIN: My plan—failed. He's right;
It was my plan. All my plans—!

POLICHINELLE: What's this? [*after putting his hand to a wet patch on the floor*]

PIERROT: Blood—blood!

O Polichinelle, Polichinelle!

Pantaloon—Pantaloon is dead

And I killed him.

POLICHINELLE: Pantaloon?

Pantaloon's dead?

PIERROT: Dead. Dead;

That's his blood; and I killed him.

POLICHINELLE: That's his blood? —That's his blood?

[*smelling his fingers*]

That's wine—yes, it's wine!

HARLEQUIN: It's what?

POLICHINELLE: Red wine.

Did he bleed that?

HARLEQUIN: Wait a minute!

Let me look—it *is* wine!

How could he bleed all that wine?

Look at that—will you look at that!

A wineskin's hidden under his coat

—The wineskin that the innkeeper gave him!

That's what you stabbed; that's what bled.

He isn't dead—he's dead drunk!

Up with you, you old scoundrel, you!

PIERROT: Pantaloon!

POLICHINELLE: Pantaloon!

HARLEQUIN: There's a tragic hero for you!

Lying there—playing dead

So he could hog it all for himself!

PANTALOON: Didn't mean . . . be unsociable . . .

But wineskin . . . wineskin leakin' badly . . .

Had to drink it fast or waste it . . .

HARLEQUIN: That was heroic of you, wasn't it?

You're a fine hero—I don't think!

PANTALOON: What'd you mean—not heroic?

You ever drink up a whole wineskin?

You ever *try* drink up a wineskin?

Me—I rose to the occasion . . . [*collapses*]

Strenuous thing . . . being heroic . . .

HARLEQUIN: [*bitterly*] Even fools make a fool of me!

Up with you—up! It can't end like this!

I can't let it end like this!

PIERROT: He's asleep. Let him sleep.

He *was* heroic.

HARLEQUIN: Failed; failed;
Failed in everything I tried;
Only the old comedy again:
Everybody unhappy with the happy ending.
[*He retrieves his hat, replaces it on his head.*]
I did no better than Fate or God,
It's really very humiliating . . .
I wish that the whole universe
And every living thing within it
Was one cockroach—just one cockroach;
I'd stamp on it—stamp on it—and be finished.
POLICHINELLE: Harlequin, you filthy swine,
What on earth were you trying to do?
PIERROT: Let him alone. Can't you see
He's in that fit of his again?
You'll get no answer from him now,
No more than you would from Fate.
Let him alone. Let him alone.
POLICHINELLE: My God, listen to that rain.
It keeps on like a waterfall.
What'll we do now?
PIERROT: We could play cards . . .
Although I haven't my spectacles
And can't tell a spade from a club.
POLICHINELLE: It won't matter. Let's play.
Only I wonder—I wonder—
PIERROT: What?
POLICHINELLE: Do you think that we could possibly play
Without using—the Queen of Hearts?
Curtain

FOUR

Olson's Penny Arcade

Is live here Ivan Ivanov
No he live de nex flur hup

I. *How the Spy was Caught*

Master of all languages
The dog had meant to speak in Goose
But slipped and spoke in Duck instead

II. *Carnival*

Lean from this balcony and look
Gaze over the crowds and see
How many guises Fate can wear

III. *Autobiography*

I walk the streets of a strange city
Streets dark as passages in dreams
Thieves rob me at each step I take
They stole my youth some ten blocks back

IV. *Macbeth*

Nothing gives such a sense of fact
As an irrevocable act

V. *Clock*

The clock ticks like a bomb
The Event will go off when

VI. *Oedipus and the Sphinx: What Really Happened*

"Man is the answer to all questions
But only if the answerer
Knows what such an answer means"
Alas poor Swellfoot did not know
And still she ravages the world
And shall until her riddle's solved

VII. *Message from Inner Space*

The bottle found in a message
Contained a sea said the man
With stars in his stomach

VIII. *Rellstab and Beethoven*

The Master kept his chamber-pot
Underneath his piano but
The perfumed parvenu did not

IX. *Helpfulness*

How helpful everybody was
To the frail old foreigner
With all those heavy suitcases
Containing germs and atom bombs

X. *Soul and Body*

The fat man much too fat to dance
Played Chopin waltzes exquisitely
The thin were much too fat to dance them

XI. *Point of View*

All the while Praxiteles
Chiselled out his masterpiece
The marble bitterly complained
That it was being mutilated

XII. *Love Story*

Long long after the rose
The thorns the thorns remain

XIII. *Advice*

"Physician heal thyself"
"Doctor yourself have a fool for a patient"

XIV. *Who's Who*

He searched for his identity
And found out he was someone else

XV. *Gnothe Seauton*

If only I knew myself well enough
To call myself by my first name . . .

XVI. *The Center*

If you sail upon the sea
You are the center of that sea

XVII. *Olson's Theory of Relativity*

Beneath your clumsy foot the ant
Is you beneath an L F Ant

XVIII. *The Rule*

I came to a country of the blind
All all were blind I asked them why
It was the rule we all obeyed
What rule I asked An eye for an eye

XIX. *Life, How to Live*

The thing to do
Said the stone in the meadow
Is to stand firm
Stay perfectly still
Content with your shadow
The thing to do
Said the water in the stream
Is to let yourself go
Flow flow
Never be still
The thing to do
Said the oak on the hill
Is to get a good grip
On the ground but be willing
To bend with the wind
And part with a leaf or a branch if you have to

But I who may not
Be still and have not
A place to go cannot
Get a good grip
Am unwilling to bend
And will give up nothing
I still do not know

The stone's covered over
The stream's drained away
The oak bent too far
Parted with too much
That's all I know

Now the thing to do
Said the wind in the pine-forest . . .

XX. *Why? Why.*

—So the fairy princess had syphilis, and the fairy prince
Was just that, et cetera, et cetera;
What of it? I say, there is still good in the world;
I say, some innocence still survives; take Snow-White
For instance; after all those years
She left the House of the Seven Dwarfs still a virgin,
Maidenhead still intact—only seven little dents in it.

XXI. *Dirty Peep-show*

All I
See
Is my
Reflected
Eye

XXII. *Blue Film*

Think of them as skeletons
Thinking of those skeletons
Think of the inane machines
Kids make with their Erector sets

XXIII. *Censorship*

A naughty goldfish draws and scrawls
Things on the aquarium walls
A much embarrassed snail erases
All but some tantalizing traces

XXIV. *Command*

Fire all the philosophers
Kick all the theologians out
The flagellant alone has found
A reasonable excuse for pain

XXV. *Last Word*

If life's a joke in all good fun
I never saw the point, for one
As for this smile you see me wear
The undertaker stitched it there

XXVI. *Winter Moon*

How still the moon is
Watching the wild turbulence
Of earthly waters

XXVII. *Fog*

Fog is the color of despair
Look the fog is everywhere

XXVIII. *Little Elegy*

The star is dead
Its light lives on

XXIX. *The Wheel*

Having tried every subterfuge
At last we disguised the battleship as a battleship
The wheel of our falsity came full circle and turned truth

XXX. *Observation*

Heights are not everything
Fuji is not beautiful from the top

XXXI. *Butterfly*

The butterfly that lived a single day
Felt it had lived a full and happy life

XXXII. *For the Blossom*

Brilliant the blossom
The dark roots that fashioned it
Never will see it

XXXIII. *Star*

Thou seest me not
          Immortal jewel of night
But I see thee
          Shine on and see me not
Shine on shine on
          Have no concern but light

Caught, like you, in the web
Of a bad winter, I
Remember and admire you:
One action upon impulse
And you were free,
And winter turned to spring.
What a sorry fault,
Thinking ourselves trapped
By work or season, when
It is we who flower
Or fail to flower; our one
Work, that flowering.
Who would not choose to see,
Rather than winter's
Chill confectionery,
A dark-blue velvet bee
Big as a walnut, or
That tiny knight of yours,
A hornet in violet armor
Hard as a crab's,
That mantis, fresh, translucent
As a leaf in spring;
Even, perhaps,
Those bombinating gnats?
To say nothing of jungle trees
Like piers supporting night,
Coiling rivers where
Alligators drift
With open jaws, and plumed
Grasses, falls of flowers.
Truly to choose
Is to act on choice; then
The winter murk dissolves,
Skies alter, the ship
Glides on foam, with glowing
Clouds beneath the keel,

Flying-fish start up
And arch away, like silver
Locusts, and we sail
Halcyon oceans where
All the islands are
Green cones capped with cloud.
—But to make the imagined
A substantial thing,
Its substance must come from ourselves;
No, spring cannot be
Unless we make the spring.

A Restaurant in South-East Asia

Nightwind: strung lanterns
Toss on the terrace.
In plunging shadows of palm and bamboo
People talk, laugh, eat, tease the carp in the lily-pond
With petals and crumbs.
Not one of them sees
How, from the broken drain
By the pink brick wall quivering with orchids,
A rat writhes out,
Hairs clotted to quills,
Beaded filth
Still glistening on him, dredged
From the secret wilderness
Beneath the bright city:
The dark wilderness
Always secret
Beneath all bright cities.

How quickly the wilderness, driven out,
Strikes back;
Seizes all we break,
Snatches all left unguarded;
Returns in all guises
—Webs sealing the shut gate,
Weeds where a house was,
Foam where a ship was,
Nightwind at the lanterns
—A rat from a drain,
Hunched, to stare at the
Strangeness
Of talking creatures,
Lights high in air,
The bright murmurous city
Flaunting fronds and flowers
Over the wilderness.

Through tiny eyes
In the sharp animal mask
Glares the great enemy
Not to be appeased:
Who, slain, always rises,
Who will not rest
Till erupting jungles uproot all towers,
Thundering mountains grind all walls down,
Till the last city
Sinks, to be
With all that has been
And will not be again:
Till what is, is wilderness.

Reflections on Mirrors

For Richard McKeon
—θειότερόν τι καὶ ἀπαθές—

I

A mirror copies everything it sees
And only thus can be the thing it is.

One mirror mirrors only what it can.
Two mirrors can reflect infinity.

A broken mirror becomes many mirrors.
Broken, it mirrors what it could not, whole.

A mirror hanging in an empty house
Reflects that emptiness, and is not empty.

A mirror suspended in the absolute Void
Would be filled with the reflection of that Void.

A mirror left in darkness reflects darkness;
Truth, then, is something other than the light.

II

Cloud-like, the seasons pass, reflected here.
This, reflecting them, is of no season.

The roaring world is silent in the mirror;
Things move in the mirror; it is motionless.

All that ranting drama become dumbshow,
Gesticulation of phantoms; nothing more.

III

To see in silence all that passes by,
And when it goes, dismiss all memory of it;

Reflect at once the fire and the ice,
At once the land, the sea; be both, and neither;

To be a surface, yet contain a depth;
Bounded by dimensions, yet unbounded;

The Place of Forms: one Form, all forms, none;
Paradox of the Many made the One;

Pure act of contemplation, of the actual only,
The single act accomplished without motion.

IV

How clear, how softly luminous its world.
To seek to enter is to shatter it.

Its only secrets candor and serenity,
Learned only by the candid and serene:

Sky-colored lakes, glazed streams, polished ice,
Prisms of rain; star-imprisoning dews,

The tranquil sea; diamond; diamond tears;
The mirroring eyes; the mirror of the mind.

The Old Man in the Tropical Aviary

Here, among palms and tree-ferns, brilliant birds
Fly back and forth through tapestries of leaves,
Perch beside blooms fantastic as themselves.
Parrots, parakeets, macaws, toucans
—There's a white crested cockatoo; there, near the glass dome,
Atop that orchid-tree, a snowy heron
Motionless, lost in thought.
How tranquil it is here!
The very air breathes tranquillity
As it does earth-odor, fern-spice, water-freshness, flower-
    fragrance.
You might think this an Eden, out of Time,
Yet, like this winding streamlet, Time runs on:
A seed drops, a root stirs, a flower expands,
And one leaf falls, another leaf unfurls.

Are Time and Death, then, even in Paradise?
No matter; it is no less Paradise.
What perishes wholly? All that is
Ceases to be, only to be again;
The fallen leaf becomes the exalted bough.
O may I be, when I again must be,
Not this forever pondering, forever puzzled thing
Pulled this way and that by reason and desire
But, say, a bird ignorant of its name,
        that yet knows what it is, what it must do,
A seed that bides its own time, to be what it must,
A root content to work in darkness, building what it never
    shall see,
A flower that lives out its whole span in silence,
A leaf that knows when its end is accomplished, and then falls.

City

City arisen by an inland sea,
Those who founded you could not foretell
The city still to be,
Nor yet can we:

A city is not habitation only
Nor power and pride made visible in stone
Nor wall or spire however sheer and bright.
All that we build is mortal as ourselves:
Not so the informing spirit, known
Only as it seeks new eminence and light.

Bridge, portal, street—all ways that link and bind—
Of what undivined
Union and communion of mankind
Are you the token, and the first surmise?
With what profound
First chord preluding hymns as yet unsung
Do all these ringing avenues resound?

Of what vast temple are these surging towers
Foundation only, and first altar-stones?

City arisen as in
Exaltation of high prophecy,
O work of man,

Declare what man shall be.

Puerto Vallarta

Day begins, not with the sun,
Nor with cock-crow, for the cocks crow at all hours,
But with a rocket spurting from a church
To burst cloud-high. The bang awakens
A bell, which clanks itself to sleep again.
Go out, now, on the chill balcony:
Beyond the palms, great shadowy rings of birds
Are turning in silence over pallid waters,
Some ritual as old as birds and dawn.
Here the west brightens first; at last the sun,
Which has had to climb a jungle-covered mountain,
Lights the town.

The town is simple enough:
Mostly white boxes with tiled roofs. Its sounds establish it
As certainly inhabited
By chickens, pigs, burros, cats, dogs,
Land- and sea-birds, as well as people; all active
According to their kind. The town does not stop at the ocean
But generously includes it
As a sort of patio. The ocean, however,

Remains itself, while pretending to be everything else,
Ceaselessly casting its nets upon the shore,
Lifting harsh hackles, rolling in dragon-coils,
Smoothing out to taut silk, carving in cloudy jade,
Or idly mirroring boats, clouds, birds.
Sunset stains the beaches black and red,
Gulls flare above the boys cleaning the catch.
At dark the hills glitter like Christmas trees,
The wind's spiced, like airs off Orient ports,
Music and laughter drift up from the square.

All simple enough; but here,
If happiness is possible for you, you can be happy.
You are not likely to think your lot too hard
Where the burro burdened with sea-stones, accepting his burden,
Feeds on what he finds, and is content.
You will not make too much of superficial things
Where pelicans bob, indifferent to the wave,
Pondering what lies beneath,
And where a vaulting dolphin or a stranded sting-ray
Hints what the depths may hold;

You will not be mastered by what is yours, or envious of what
   is not
By an ocean that can give almost anything you want
And with the next wave, take it back again;
Where children who lack toys
Make balls of newspaper and string,
Toboggan down the cobbles on soaped boards,
Or flounder through tumbling foam. (All have at least one toy,
The biggest in the world: the Pacific.)

And it would be difficult to feel too much attachment to self
Where the sea hourly washes up relics
Of other lives that thought themselves important;
Difficult even to fear death
Where the sea-tern wrenching eagerly at a squid
Demonstrates that death is merely life changing to life,

And where the sea itself is both life and death,
Which differ only
As the wave gathering and the wave breaking,
The ship coming in by night
Like a star that becomes a cluster of stars descending,
And the ship going out like a constellation climbing
Till all its lights fuse to a single star
Rising to rejoin its fellow stars.